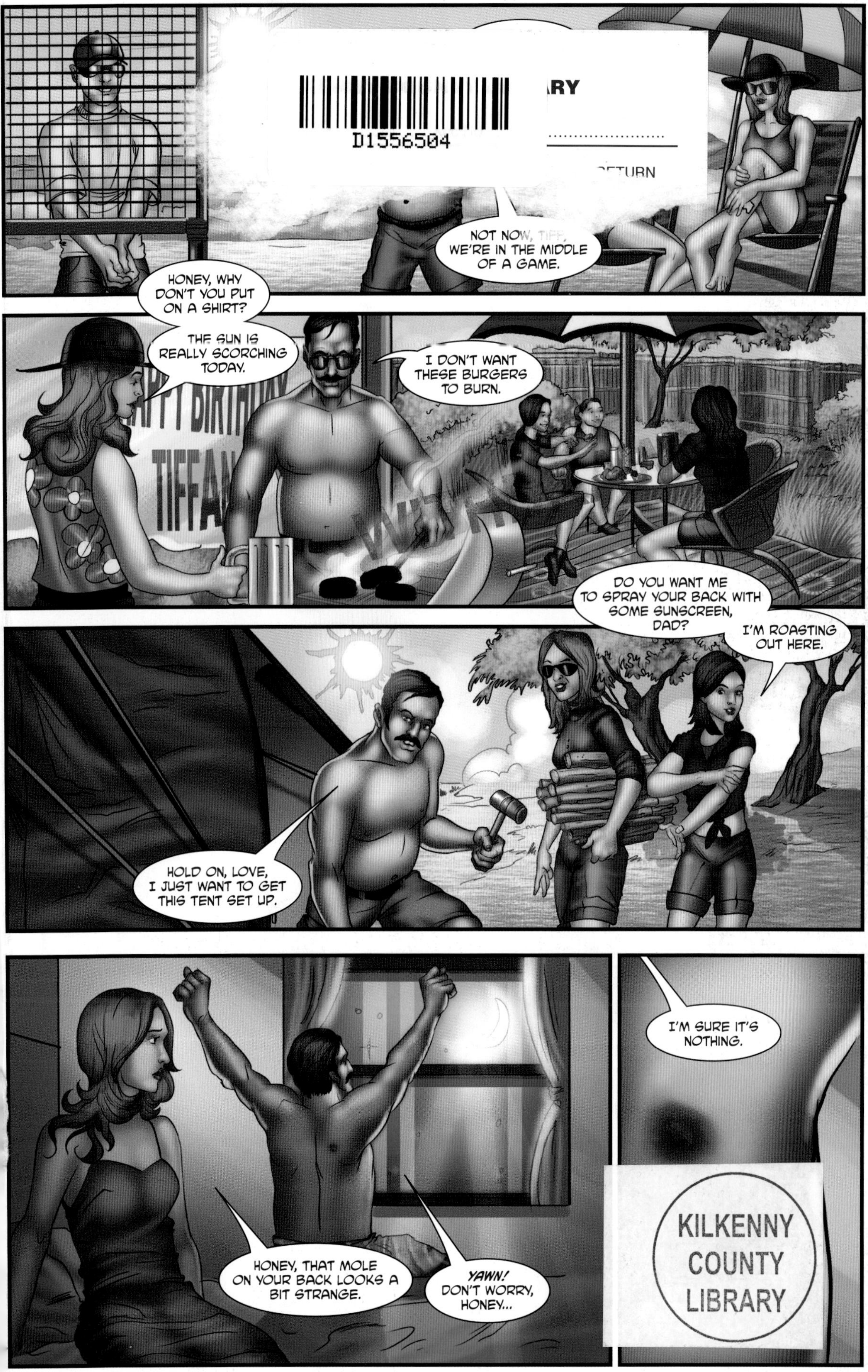
NOT NOW, TIFF, WE'RE IN THE MIDDLE OF A GAME.
HONEY, WHY DON'T YOU PUT ON A SHIRT?
THE SUN IS REALLY SCORCHING TODAY.
HAPPY BIRTHDAY TIFFAN
I DON'T WANT THESE BURGERS TO BURN.
DO YOU WANT ME TO SPRAY YOUR BACK WITH SOME SUNSCREEN, DAD?
I'M ROASTING OUT HERE.
HOLD ON, LOVE, I JUST WANT TO GET THIS TENT SET UP.
HONEY, THAT MOLE ON YOUR BACK LOOKS A BIT STRANGE.
YAWN! DON'T WORRY, HONEY...
I'M SURE IT'S NOTHING.

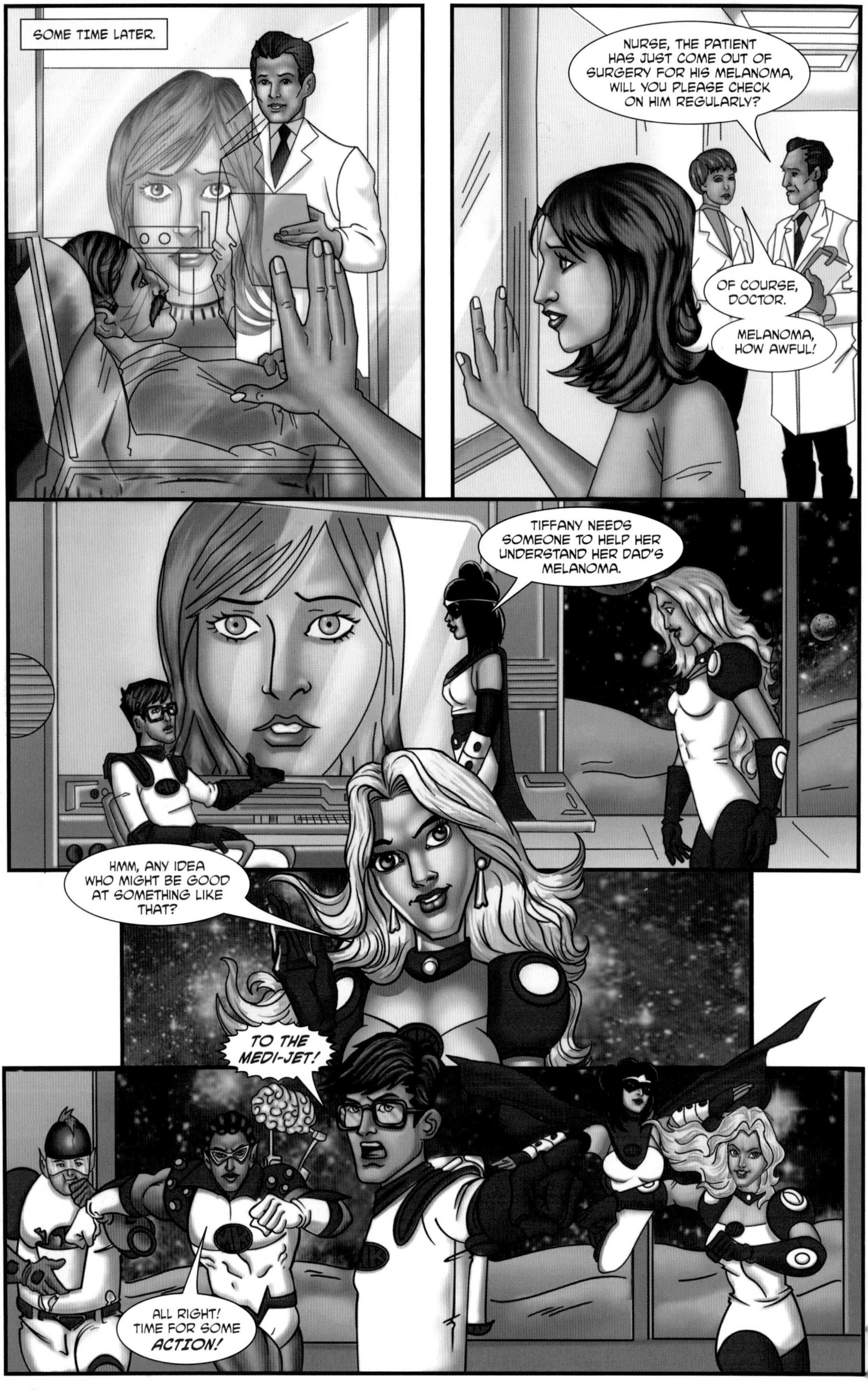
SOME TIME LATER.
NURSE, THE PATIENT HAS JUST COME OUT OF SURGERY FOR HIS MELANOMA, WILL YOU PLEASE CHECK ON HIM REGULARLY?
OF COURSE, DOCTOR.
MELANOMA, HOW AWFUL!
TIFFANY NEEDS SOMEONE TO HELP HER UNDERSTAND HER DAD'S MELANOMA.
HMM, ANY IDEA WHO MIGHT BE GOOD AT SOMETHING LIKE THAT?
TO THE MEDI-JET!
ALL RIGHT! TIME FOR SOME ACTION!

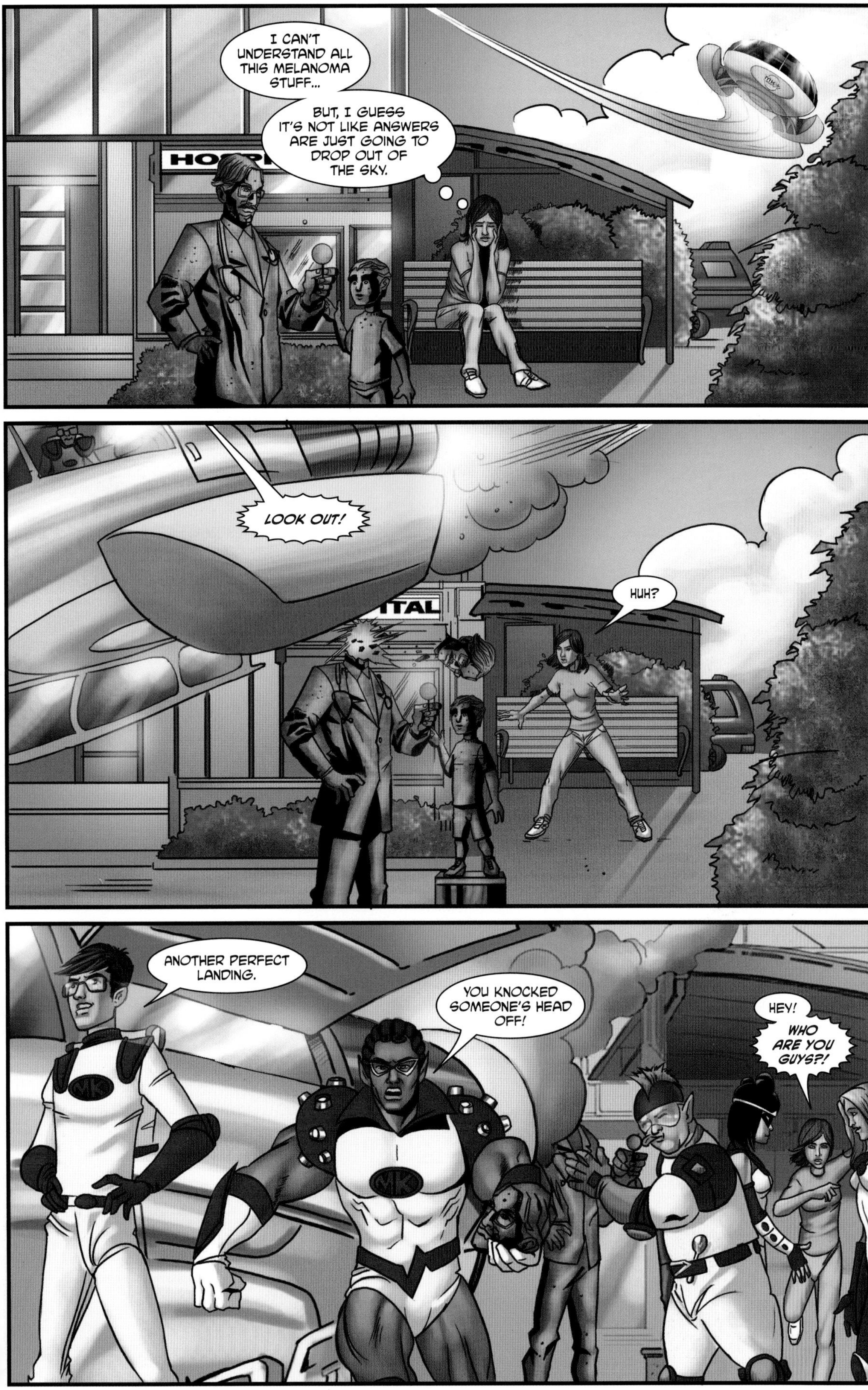
I CAN'T UNDERSTAND ALL THIS MELANOMA STUFF...
BUT, I GUESS IT'S NOT LIKE ANSWERS ARE JUST GOING TO DROP OUT OF THE SKY.
LOOK OUT!
HUH?
ANOTHER PERFECT LANDING.
YOU KNOCKED SOMEONE'S HEAD OFF!
HEY! WHO ARE YOU GUYS?!

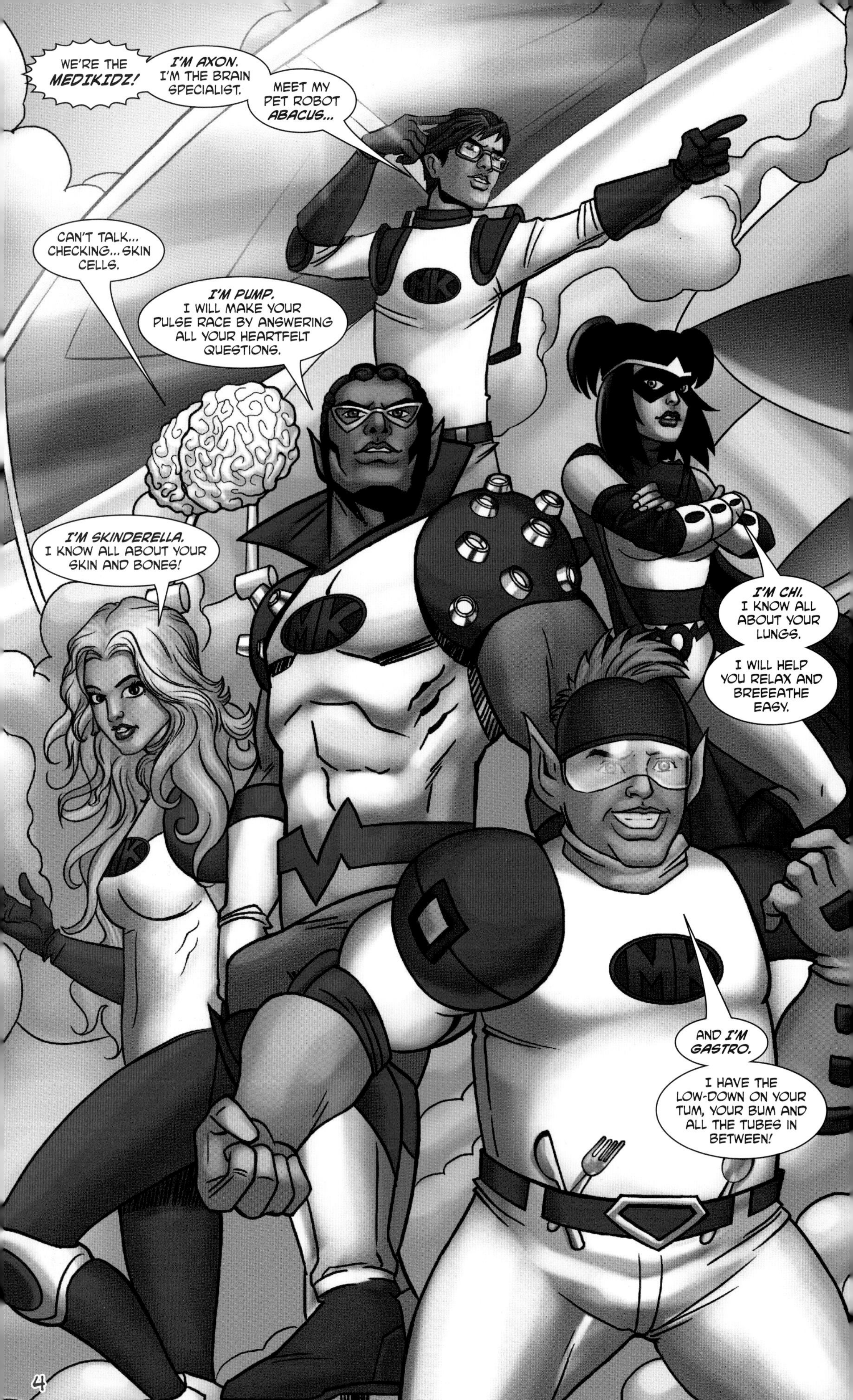
WE'RE THE MEDIKIDZ!
I'M AXON. I'M THE BRAIN SPECIALIST.
MEET MY PET ROBOT ABACUS...
CAN'T TALK... CHECKING... SKIN CELLS.
I'M PUMP. I WILL MAKE YOUR PULSE RACE BY ANSWERING ALL YOUR HEARTFELT QUESTIONS.
I'M SKINDERELLA. I KNOW ALL ABOUT YOUR SKIN AND BONES!
I'M CHI. I KNOW ALL ABOUT YOUR LUNGS.
I WILL HELP YOU RELAX AND BREEEATHE EASY.
AND I'M GASTRO.
I HAVE THE LOW-DOWN ON YOUR TUM, YOUR BUM AND ALL THE TUBES IN BETWEEN!

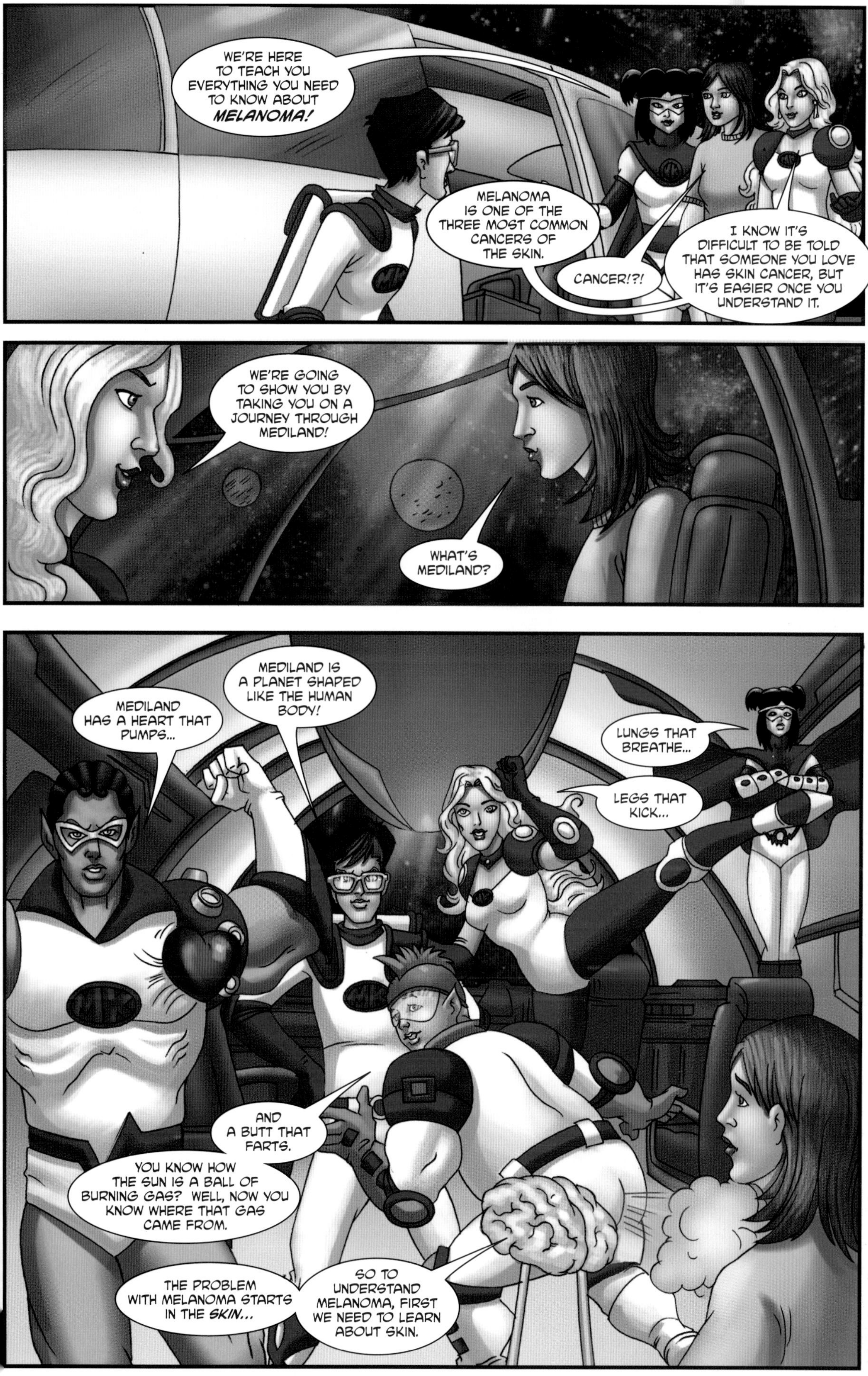
WE'RE HERE TO TEACH YOU EVERYTHING YOU NEED TO KNOW ABOUT *MELANOMA!*
MELANOMA IS ONE OF THE THREE MOST COMMON CANCERS OF THE SKIN.
CANCER!?!
I KNOW IT'S DIFFICULT TO BE TOLD THAT SOMEONE YOU LOVE HAS SKIN CANCER, BUT IT'S EASIER ONCE YOU UNDERSTAND IT.
WE'RE GOING TO SHOW YOU BY TAKING YOU ON A JOURNEY THROUGH MEDILAND!
WHAT'S MEDILAND?
MEDILAND IS A PLANET SHAPED LIKE THE HUMAN BODY!
MEDILAND HAS A HEART THAT PUMPS...
LUNGS THAT BREATHE...
LEGS THAT KICK...
AND A BUTT THAT FARTS.
YOU KNOW HOW THE SUN IS A BALL OF BURNING GAS? WELL, NOW YOU KNOW WHERE THAT GAS CAME FROM.
THE PROBLEM WITH MELANOMA STARTS IN THE *SKIN...*
SO TO UNDERSTAND MELANOMA, FIRST WE NEED TO LEARN ABOUT SKIN.

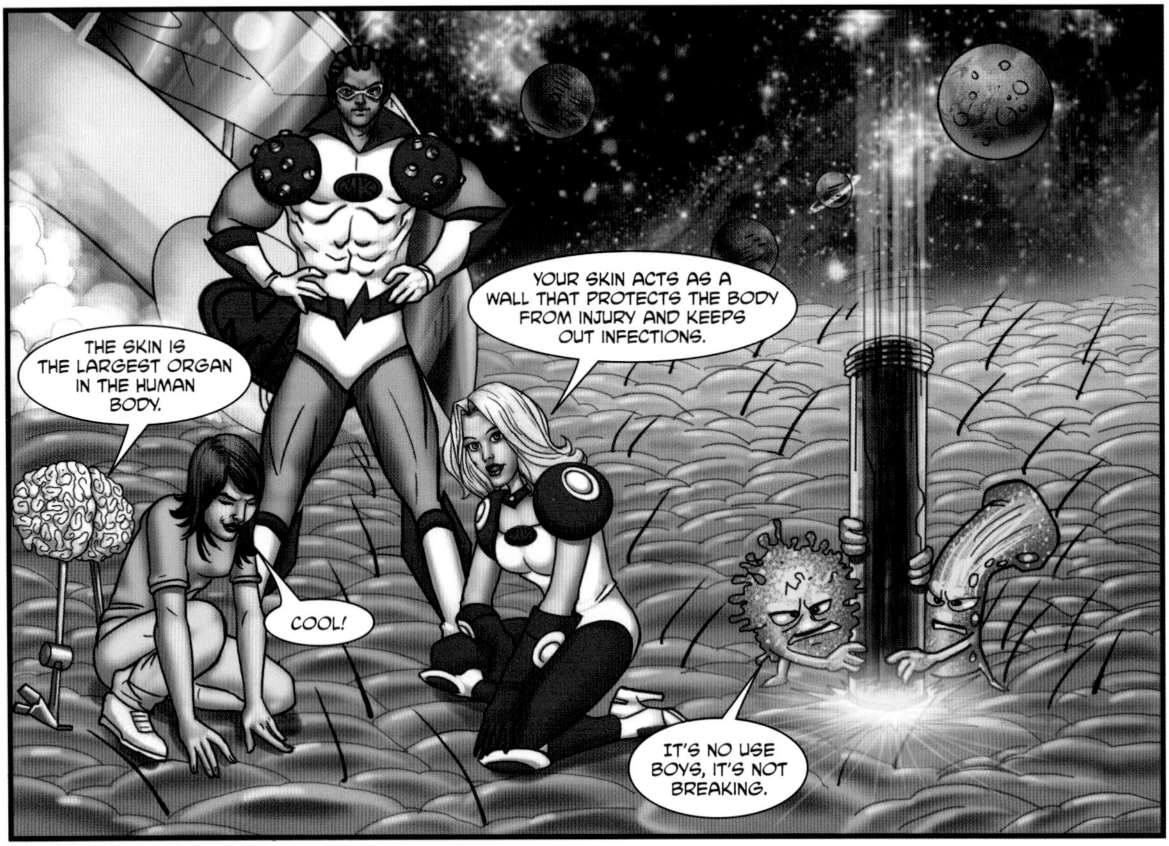
THE SKIN IS THE LARGEST ORGAN IN THE HUMAN BODY.
YOUR SKIN ACTS AS A WALL THAT PROTECTS THE BODY FROM INJURY AND KEEPS OUT INFECTIONS.
COOL!
IT'S NO USE BOYS, IT'S NOT BREAKING.

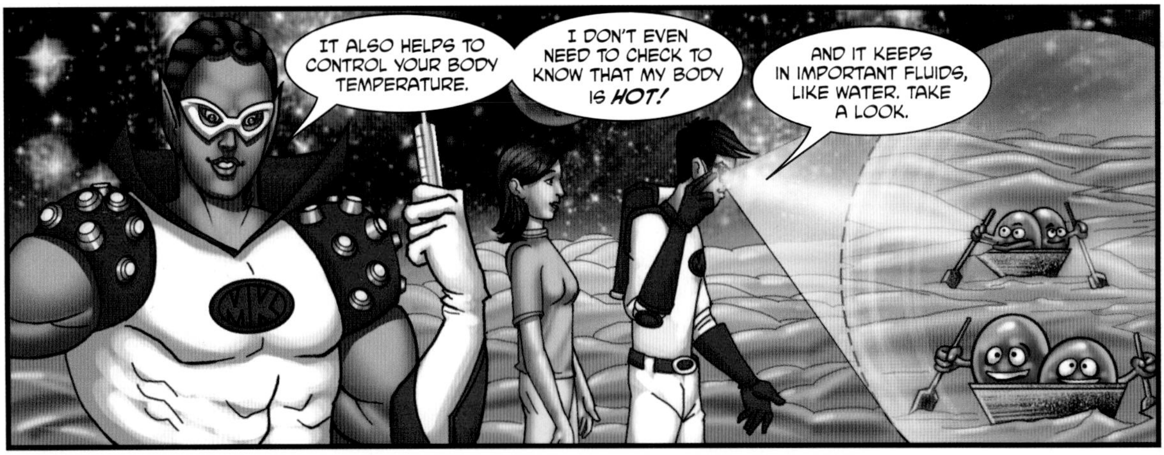
IT ALSO HELPS TO CONTROL YOUR BODY TEMPERATURE.
I DON'T EVEN NEED TO CHECK TO KNOW THAT MY BODY IS ***HOT!***
AND IT KEEPS IN IMPORTANT FLUIDS, LIKE WATER. TAKE A LOOK.

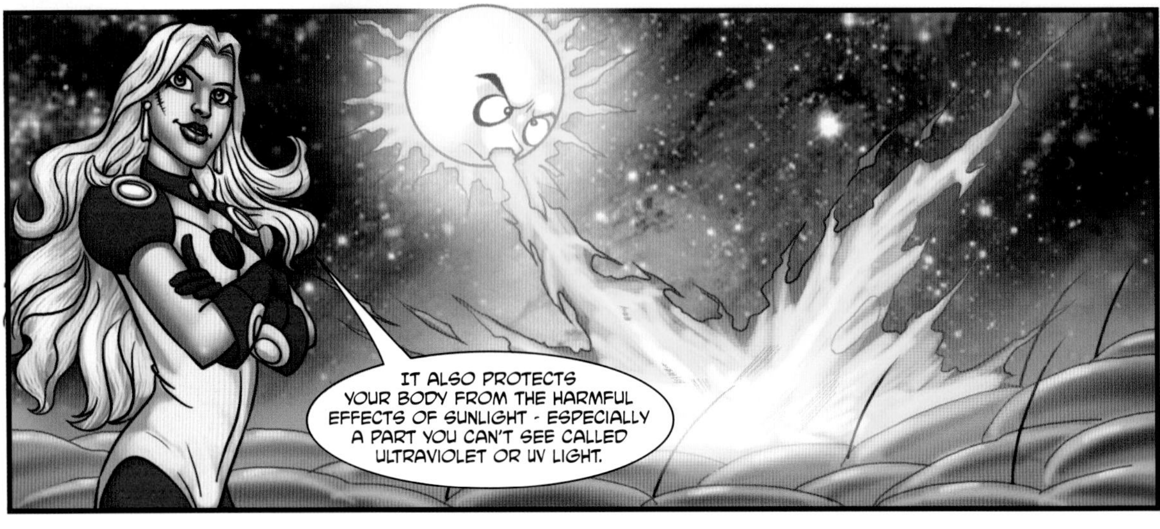
IT ALSO PROTECTS YOUR BODY FROM THE HARMFUL EFFECTS OF SUNLIGHT - ESPECIALLY A PART YOU CAN'T SEE CALLED ULTRAVIOLET OR UV LIGHT.

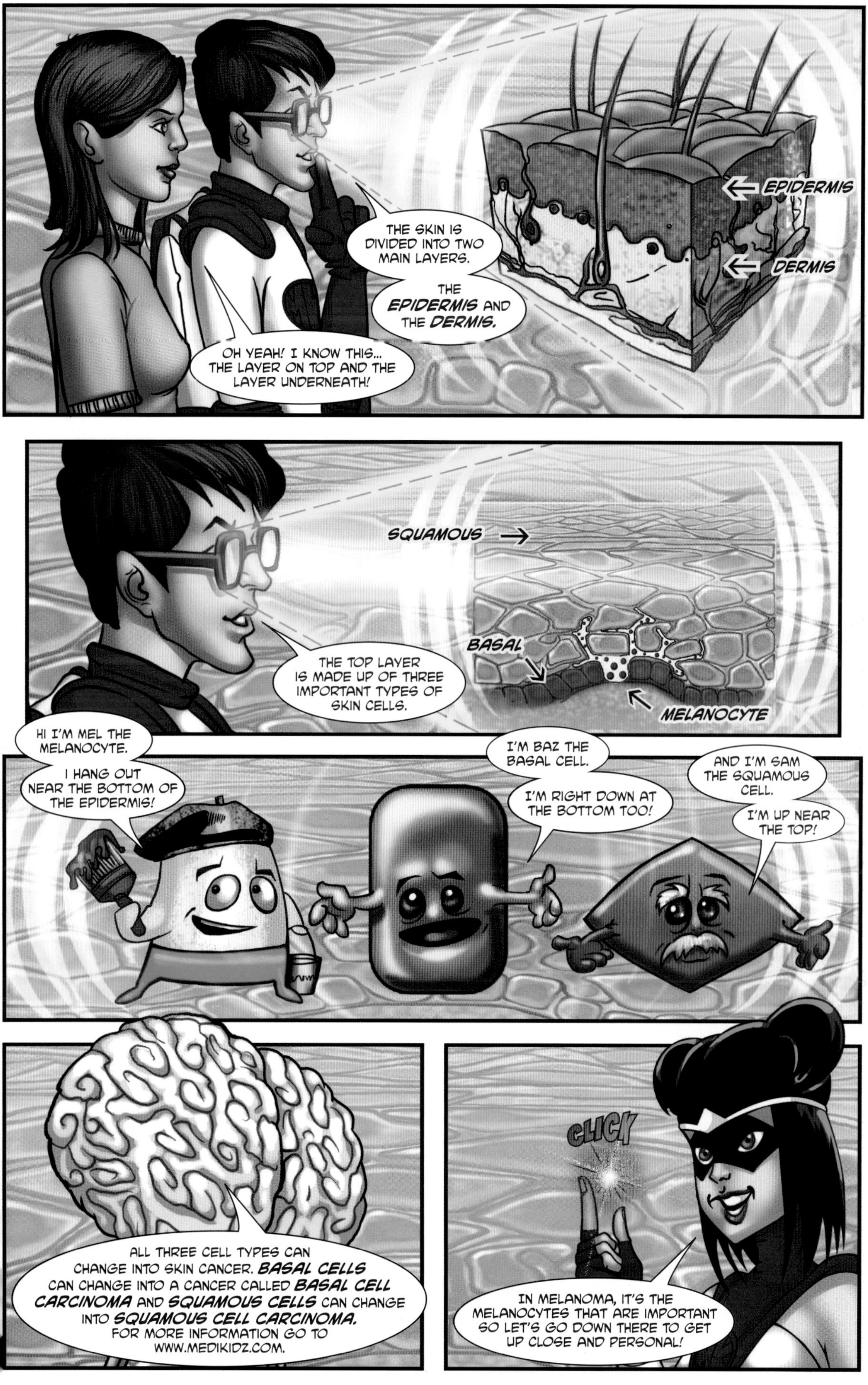
EPIDERMIS
DERMIS
THE SKIN IS DIVIDED INTO TWO MAIN LAYERS.
THE EPIDERMIS AND THE DERMIS.
OH YEAH! I KNOW THIS... THE LAYER ON TOP AND THE LAYER UNDERNEATH!
SQUAMOUS
BASAL
MELANOCYTE
THE TOP LAYER IS MADE UP OF THREE IMPORTANT TYPES OF SKIN CELLS.
HI I'M MEL THE MELANOCYTE.
I HANG OUT NEAR THE BOTTOM OF THE EPIDERMIS!
I'M BAZ THE BASAL CELL.
I'M RIGHT DOWN AT THE BOTTOM TOO!
AND I'M SAM THE SQUAMOUS CELL.
I'M UP NEAR THE TOP!
ALL THREE CELL TYPES CAN CHANGE INTO SKIN CANCER. BASAL CELLS CAN CHANGE INTO A CANCER CALLED BASAL CELL CARCINOMA AND SQUAMOUS CELLS CAN CHANGE INTO SQUAMOUS CELL CARCINOMA. FOR MORE INFORMATION GO TO WWW.MEDIKIDZ.COM.
CLICK
IN MELANOMA, IT'S THE MELANOCYTES THAT ARE IMPORTANT SO LET'S GO DOWN THERE TO GET UP CLOSE AND PERSONAL!

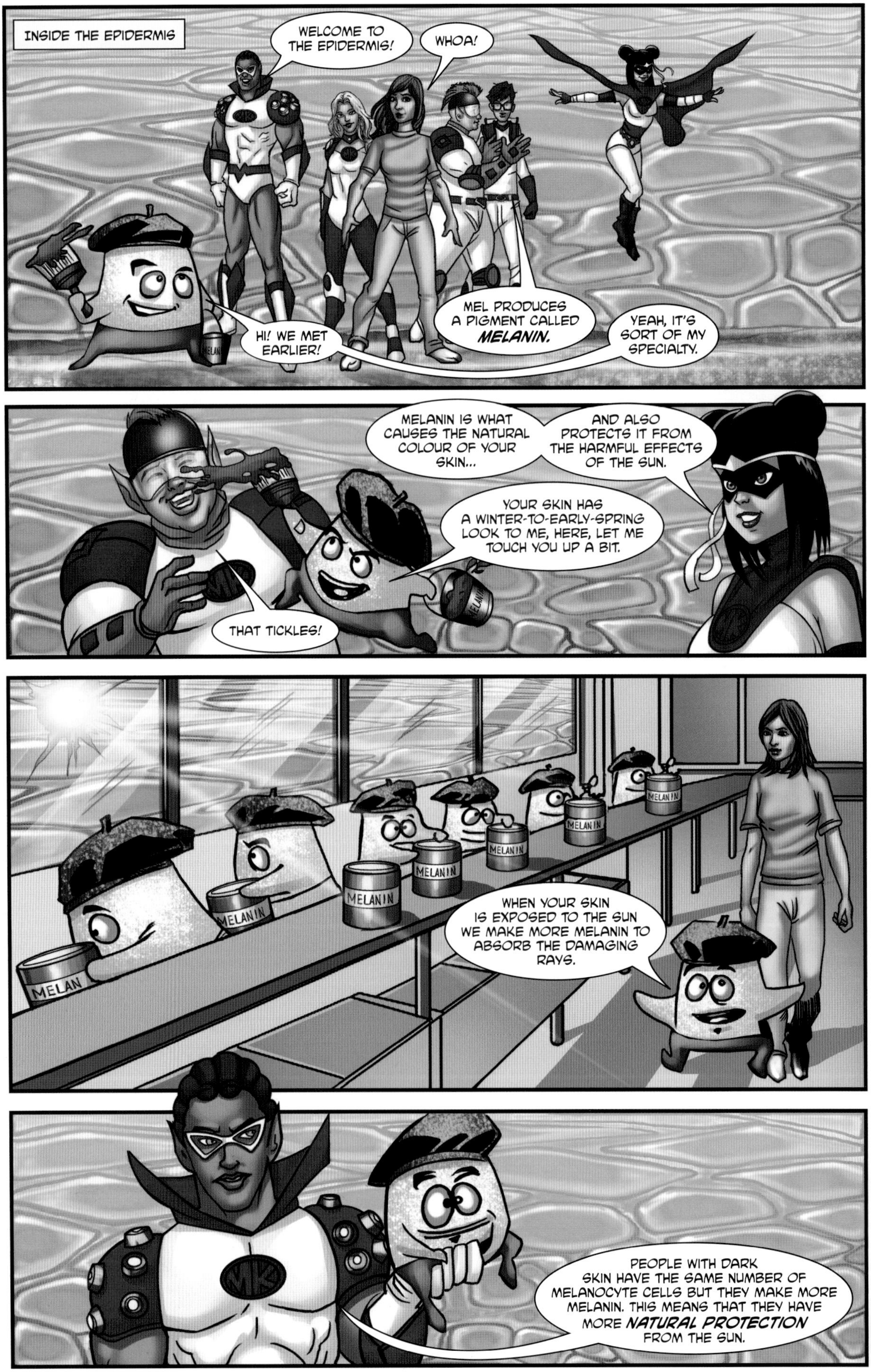
INSIDE THE EPIDERMIS
WELCOME TO THE EPIDERMIS!
WHOA!
HI! WE MET EARLIER!
MEL PRODUCES A PIGMENT CALLED MELANIN.
YEAH, IT'S SORT OF MY SPECIALTY.
MELANIN IS WHAT CAUSES THE NATURAL COLOUR OF YOUR SKIN...
AND ALSO PROTECTS IT FROM THE HARMFUL EFFECTS OF THE SUN.
YOUR SKIN HAS A WINTER-TO-EARLY-SPRING LOOK TO ME, HERE, LET ME TOUCH YOU UP A BIT.
THAT TICKLES!
WHEN YOUR SKIN IS EXPOSED TO THE SUN WE MAKE MORE MELANIN TO ABSORB THE DAMAGING RAYS.
PEOPLE WITH DARK SKIN HAVE THE SAME NUMBER OF MELANOCYTE CELLS BUT THEY MAKE MORE MELANIN. THIS MEANS THAT THEY HAVE MORE NATURAL PROTECTION FROM THE SUN.

TO DO ITS JOB PROPERLY, YOUR SKIN REPLACES ITSELF EVERY 27-30 DAYS BY SHEDDING THE TOP LAYER AND REPLACING IT WITH NEW SKIN CELLS.
GET MOVING, OLD MAN... YOUNG NEW CELLS COMING THROUGH!
BUT THERE WAS STILL SO MUCH I WANTED TO SEE!
TO REPLACE THE CELLS THAT SHED, A NORMAL HEALTHY SKIN CELL WILL COPY ITSELF BY DIVIDING...
AND THEN GROWING!
THE SKIN CELL SPLITS AND YOU HAVE ***TWO*** HEALTHY NORMAL WORKING CELLS...
WOW, I FEEL A WHOLE LOT LIGHTER!
THIS REPLACES THE OLD CELLS THAT DIE.
THIS IS WHAT ***NORMALLY*** HAPPENS IN THE EPIDERMIS.
WHAT DO YOU MEAN ***NORMALLY?!*** WHEN WOULD THIS NOT HAPPEN?
WELL, SOMETIMES THE CELLS CAN...

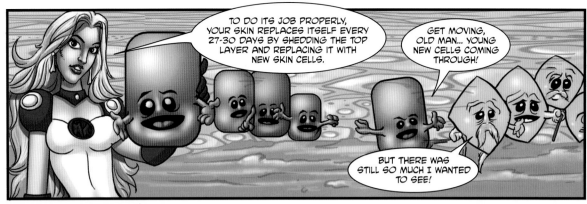

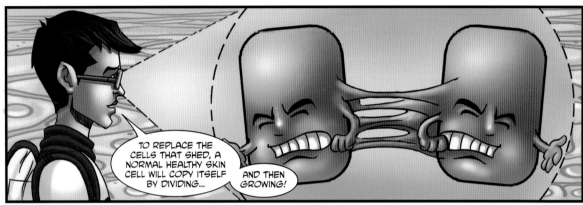

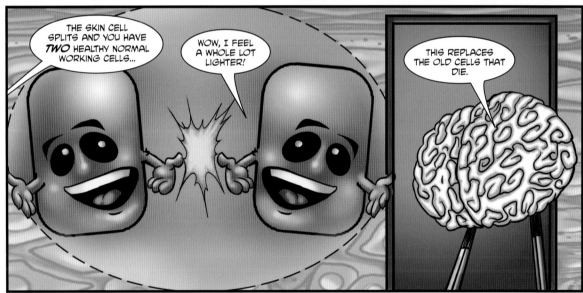

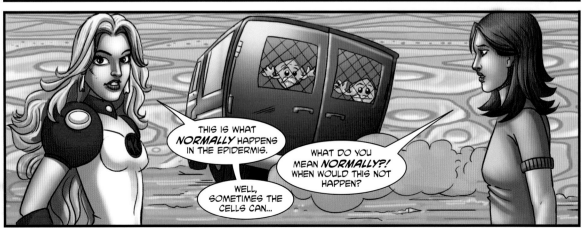

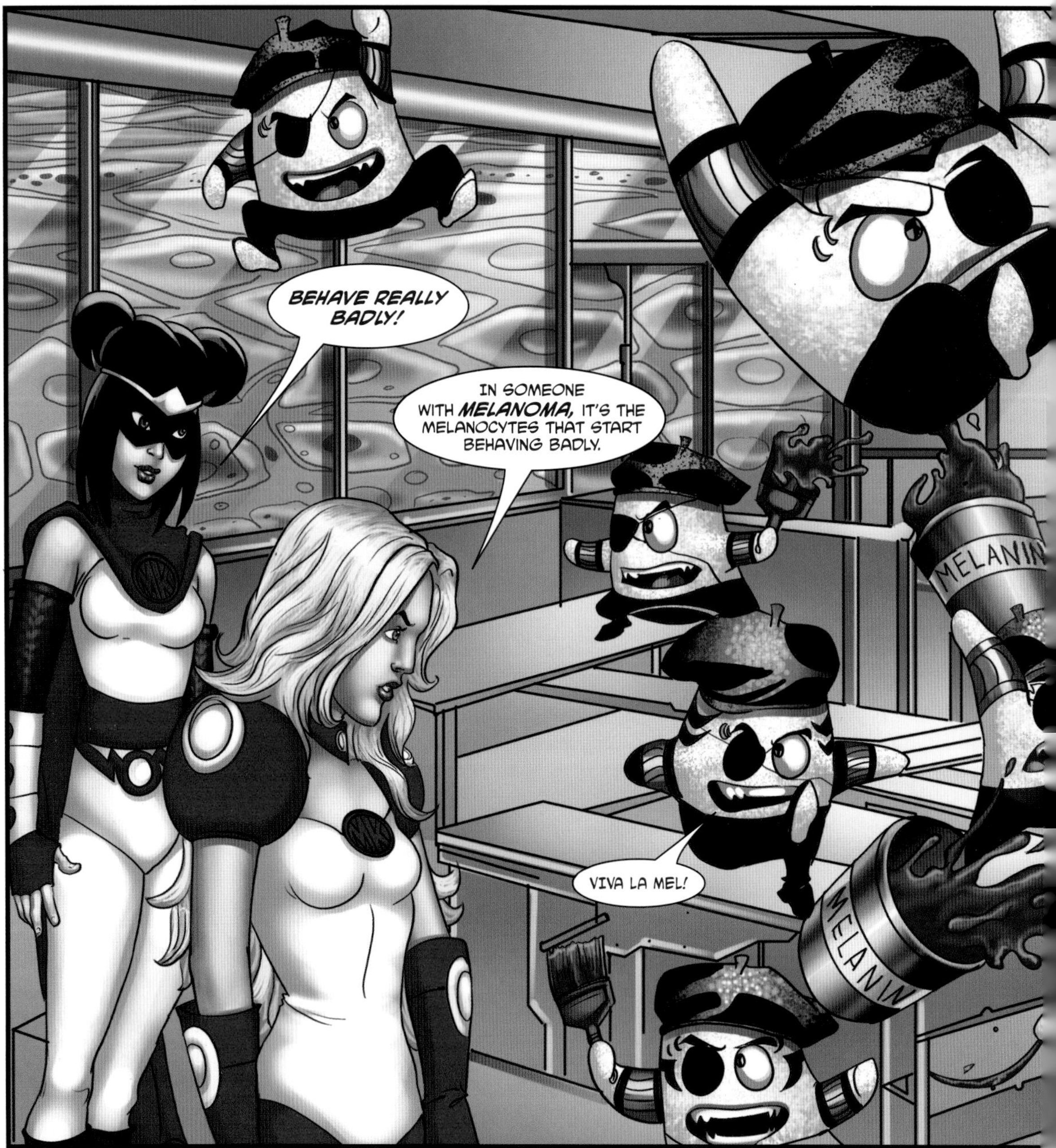
BEHAVE REALLY BADLY!
IN SOMEONE WITH MELANOMA, IT'S THE MELANOCYTES THAT START BEHAVING BADLY.
MELANIN
VIVA LA MEL!
MELANIN

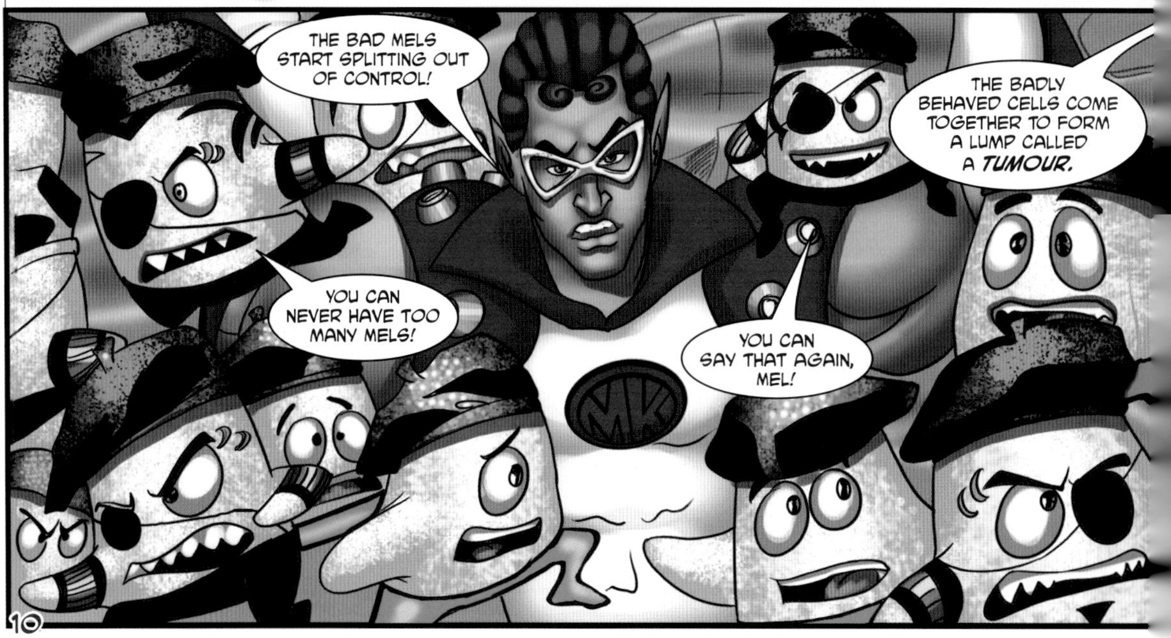
THE BAD MELS START SPLITTING OUT OF CONTROL!
THE BADLY BEHAVED CELLS COME TOGETHER TO FORM A LUMP CALLED A TUMOUR.
YOU CAN NEVER HAVE TOO MANY MELS!
YOU CAN SAY THAT AGAIN, MEL!

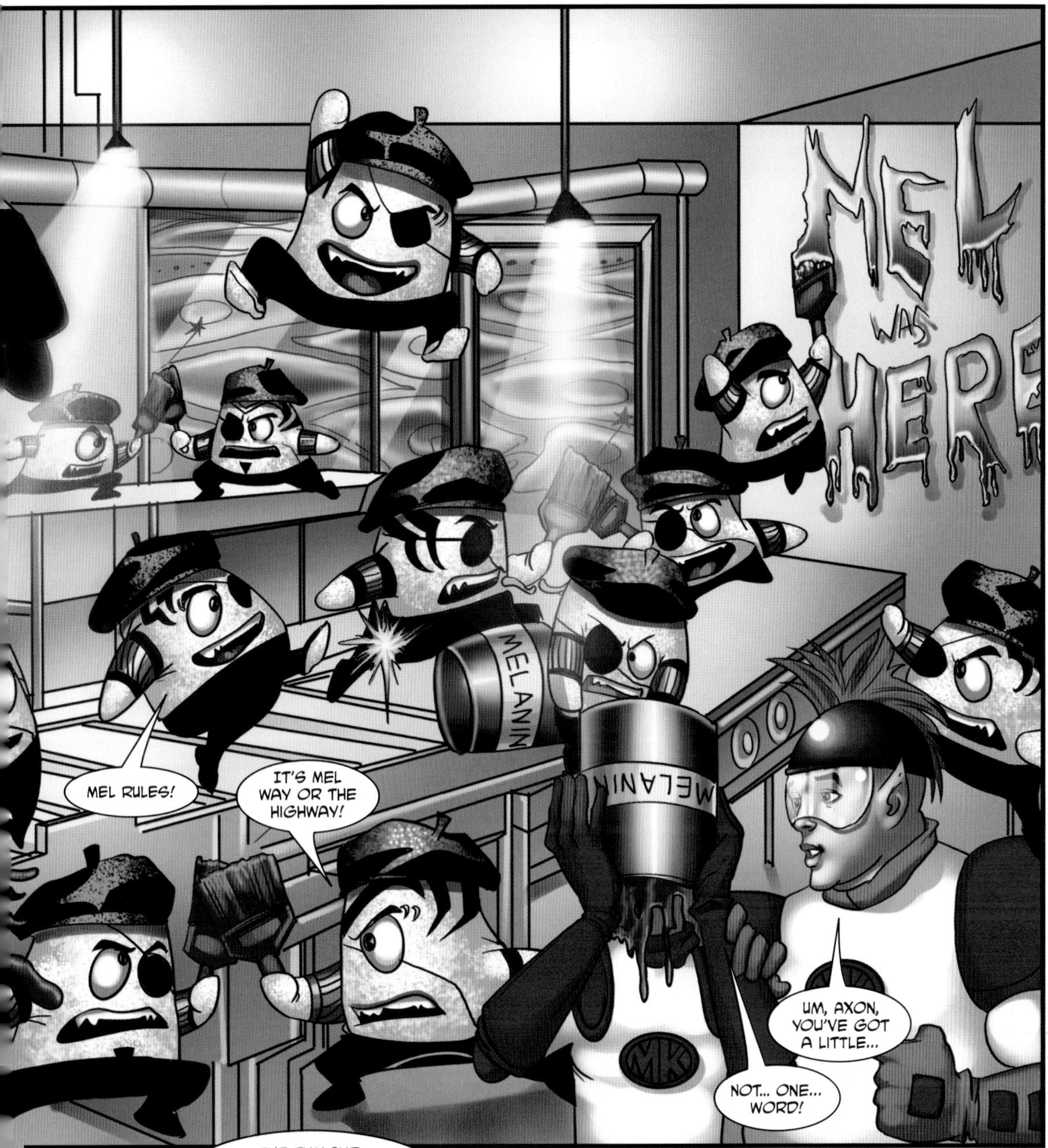
MEL WAS HERE
MELANIN
MELANIN
MEL RULES!
IT'S MEL WAY OR THE HIGHWAY!
UM, AXON, YOU'VE GOT A LITTLE...
NOT... ONE... WORD!

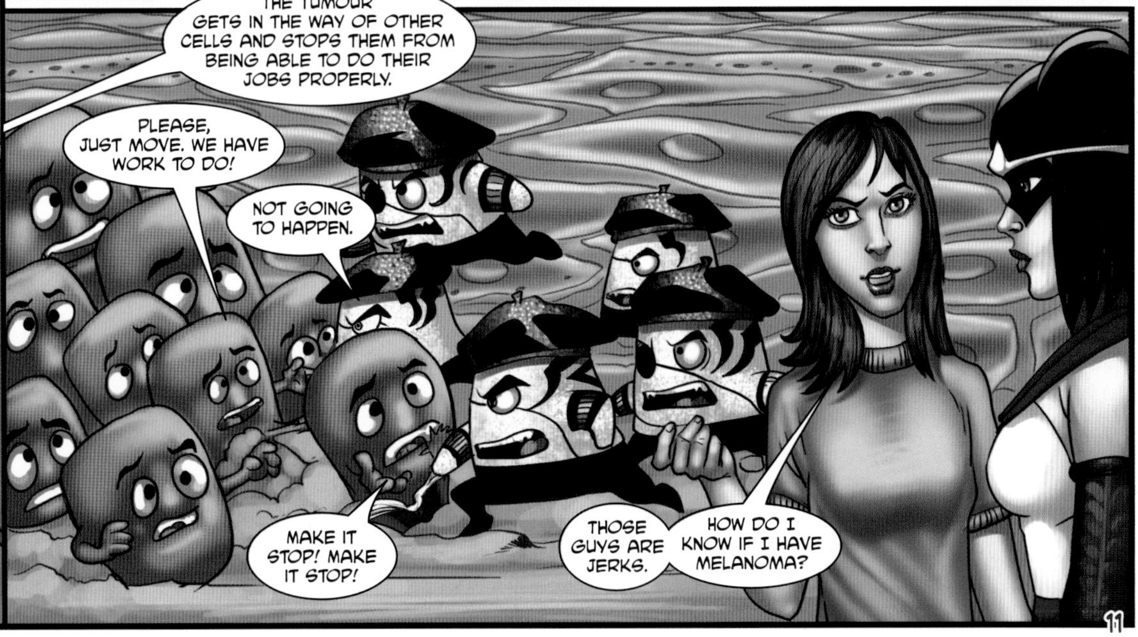
THE TUMOUR GETS IN THE WAY OF OTHER CELLS AND STOPS THEM FROM BEING ABLE TO DO THEIR JOBS PROPERLY.
PLEASE, JUST MOVE. WE HAVE WORK TO DO!
NOT GOING TO HAPPEN.
MAKE IT STOP! MAKE IT STOP!
THOSE GUYS ARE JERKS.
HOW DO I KNOW IF I HAVE MELANOMA?

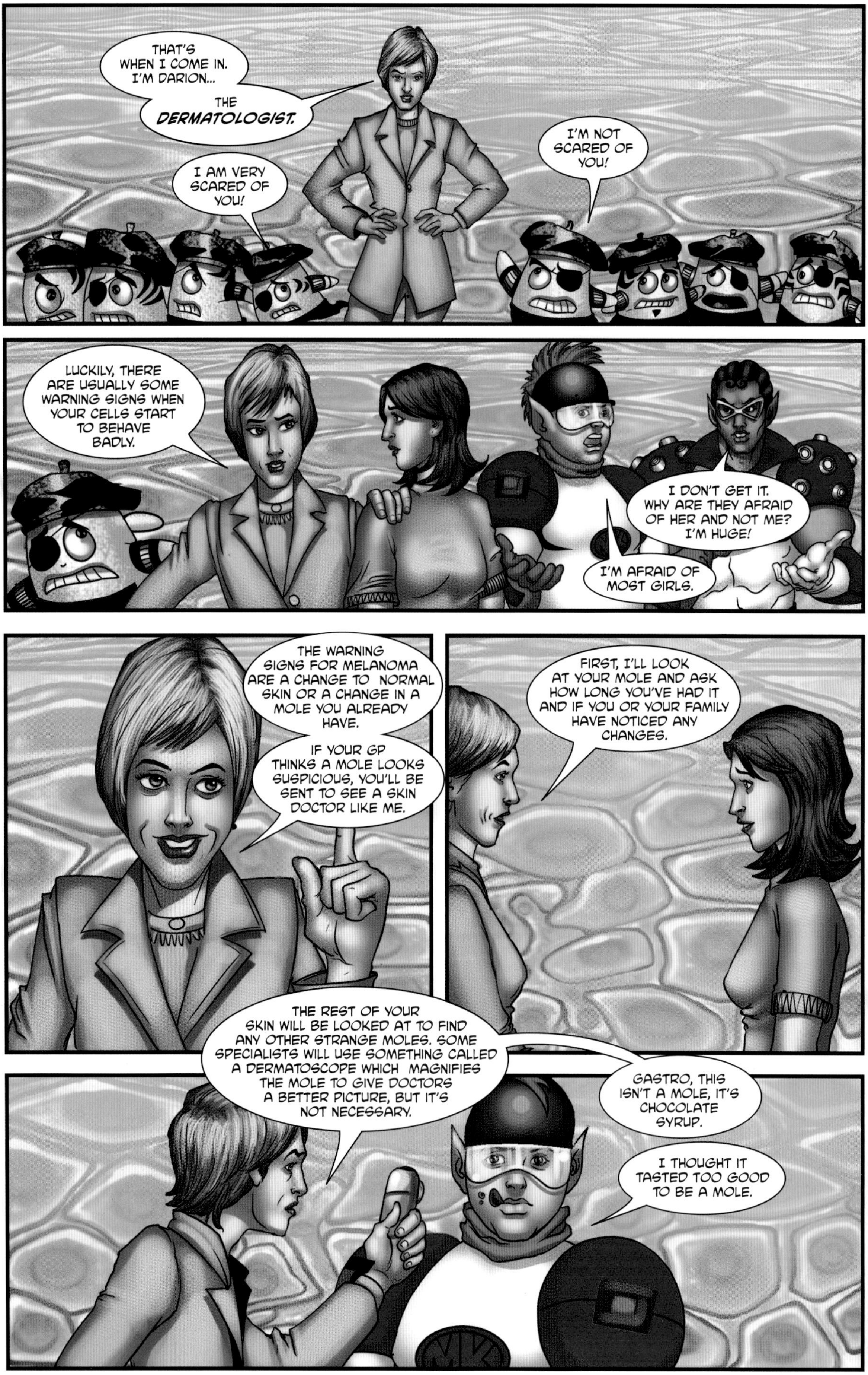
THAT'S WHEN I COME IN. I'M DARION...
THE DERMATOLOGIST.
I AM VERY SCARED OF YOU!
I'M NOT SCARED OF YOU!
LUCKILY, THERE ARE USUALLY SOME WARNING SIGNS WHEN YOUR CELLS START TO BEHAVE BADLY.
I DON'T GET IT. WHY ARE THEY AFRAID OF HER AND NOT ME? I'M HUGE!
I'M AFRAID OF MOST GIRLS.
THE WARNING SIGNS FOR MELANOMA ARE A CHANGE TO NORMAL SKIN OR A CHANGE IN A MOLE YOU ALREADY HAVE.
IF YOUR GP THINKS A MOLE LOOKS SUSPICIOUS, YOU'LL BE SENT TO SEE A SKIN DOCTOR LIKE ME.
FIRST, I'LL LOOK AT YOUR MOLE AND ASK HOW LONG YOU'VE HAD IT AND IF YOU OR YOUR FAMILY HAVE NOTICED ANY CHANGES.
THE REST OF YOUR SKIN WILL BE LOOKED AT TO FIND ANY OTHER STRANGE MOLES. SOME SPECIALISTS WILL USE SOMETHING CALLED A DERMATOSCOPE WHICH MAGNIFIES THE MOLE TO GIVE DOCTORS A BETTER PICTURE, BUT IT'S NOT NECESSARY.
GASTRO, THIS ISN'T A MOLE, IT'S CHOCOLATE SYRUP.
I THOUGHT IT TASTED TOO GOOD TO BE A MOLE.

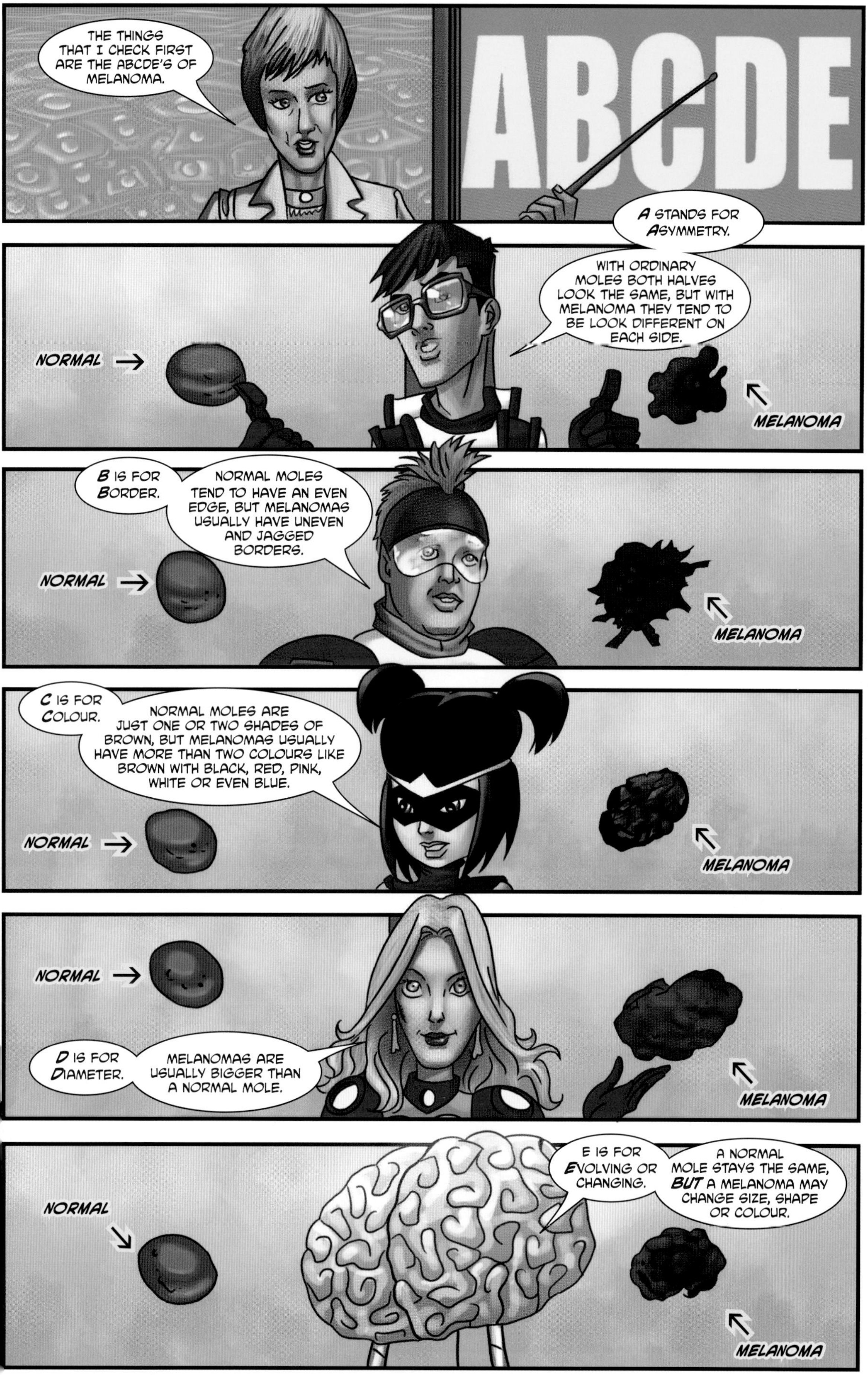
THE THINGS THAT I CHECK FIRST ARE THE ABCDE'S OF MELANOMA.
ABCDE
A STANDS FOR ASYMMETRY.
WITH ORDINARY MOLES BOTH HALVES LOOK THE SAME, BUT WITH MELANOMA THEY TEND TO BE LOOK DIFFERENT ON EACH SIDE.
NORMAL
MELANOMA
B IS FOR BORDER.
NORMAL MOLES TEND TO HAVE AN EVEN EDGE, BUT MELANOMAS USUALLY HAVE UNEVEN AND JAGGED BORDERS.
NORMAL
MELANOMA
C IS FOR COLOUR.
NORMAL MOLES ARE JUST ONE OR TWO SHADES OF BROWN, BUT MELANOMAS USUALLY HAVE MORE THAN TWO COLOURS LIKE BROWN WITH BLACK, RED, PINK, WHITE OR EVEN BLUE.
NORMAL
MELANOMA
NORMAL
D IS FOR DIAMETER.
MELANOMAS ARE USUALLY BIGGER THAN A NORMAL MOLE.
MELANOMA
E IS FOR EVOLVING OR CHANGING.
A NORMAL MOLE STAYS THE SAME, BUT A MELANOMA MAY CHANGE SIZE, SHAPE OR COLOUR.
NORMAL
MELANOMA

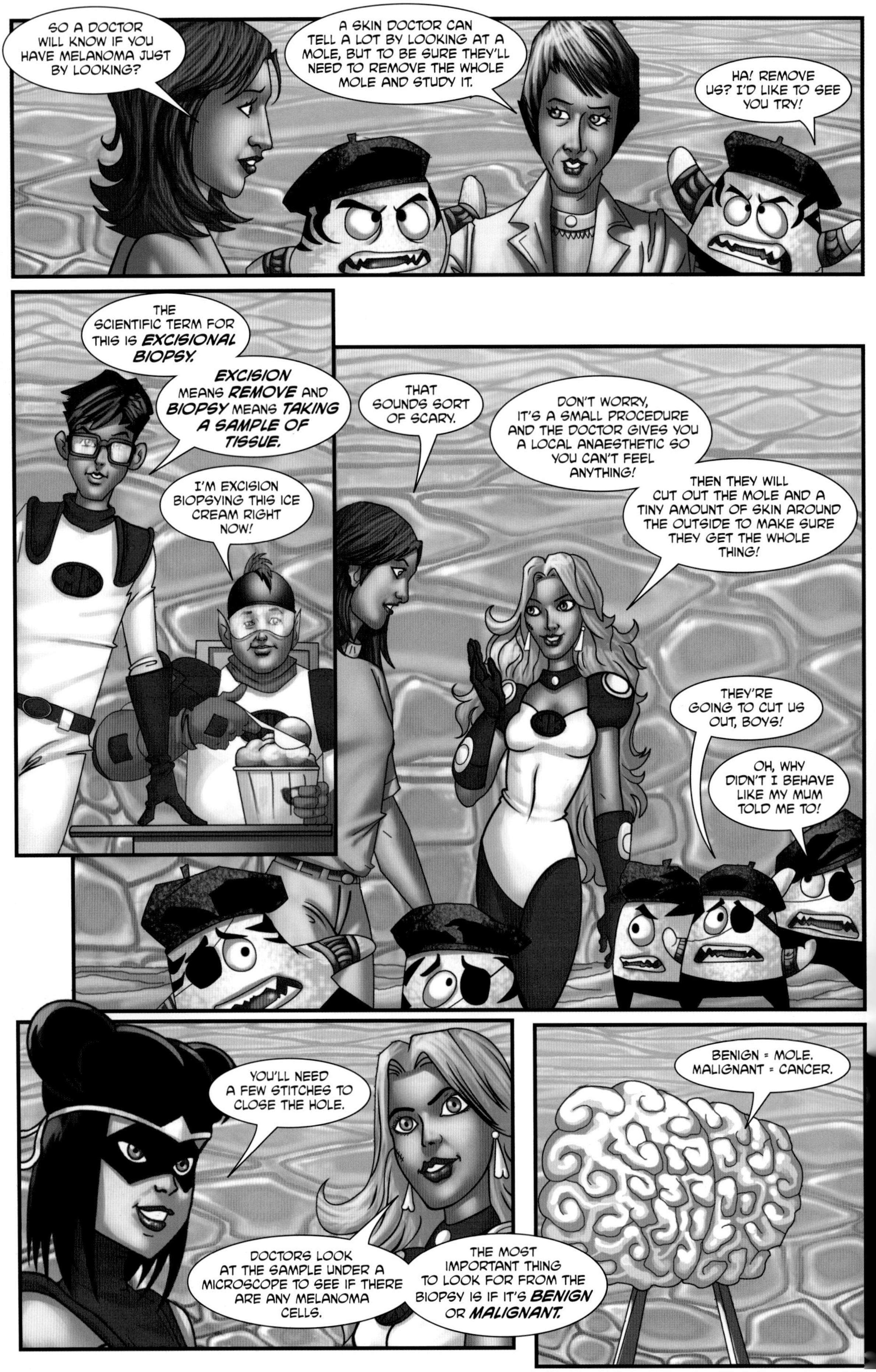
SO A DOCTOR WILL KNOW IF YOU HAVE MELANOMA JUST BY LOOKING?
A SKIN DOCTOR CAN TELL A LOT BY LOOKING AT A MOLE, BUT TO BE SURE THEY'LL NEED TO REMOVE THE WHOLE MOLE AND STUDY IT.
HA! REMOVE US? I'D LIKE TO SEE YOU TRY!
THE SCIENTIFIC TERM FOR THIS IS EXCISIONAL BIOPSY.
EXCISION MEANS REMOVE AND BIOPSY MEANS TAKING A SAMPLE OF TISSUE.
I'M EXCISION BIOPSYING THIS ICE CREAM RIGHT NOW!
THAT SOUNDS SORT OF SCARY.
DON'T WORRY, IT'S A SMALL PROCEDURE AND THE DOCTOR GIVES YOU A LOCAL ANAESTHETIC SO YOU CAN'T FEEL ANYTHING!
THEN THEY WILL CUT OUT THE MOLE AND A TINY AMOUNT OF SKIN AROUND THE OUTSIDE TO MAKE SURE THEY GET THE WHOLE THING!
THEY'RE GOING TO CUT US OUT, BOYS!
OH, WHY DIDN'T I BEHAVE LIKE MY MUM TOLD ME TO!
YOU'LL NEED A FEW STITCHES TO CLOSE THE HOLE.
DOCTORS LOOK AT THE SAMPLE UNDER A MICROSCOPE TO SEE IF THERE ARE ANY MELANOMA CELLS.
THE MOST IMPORTANT THING TO LOOK FOR FROM THE BIOPSY IS IF IT'S BENIGN OR MALIGNANT.
BENIGN = MOLE.
MALIGNANT = CANCER.

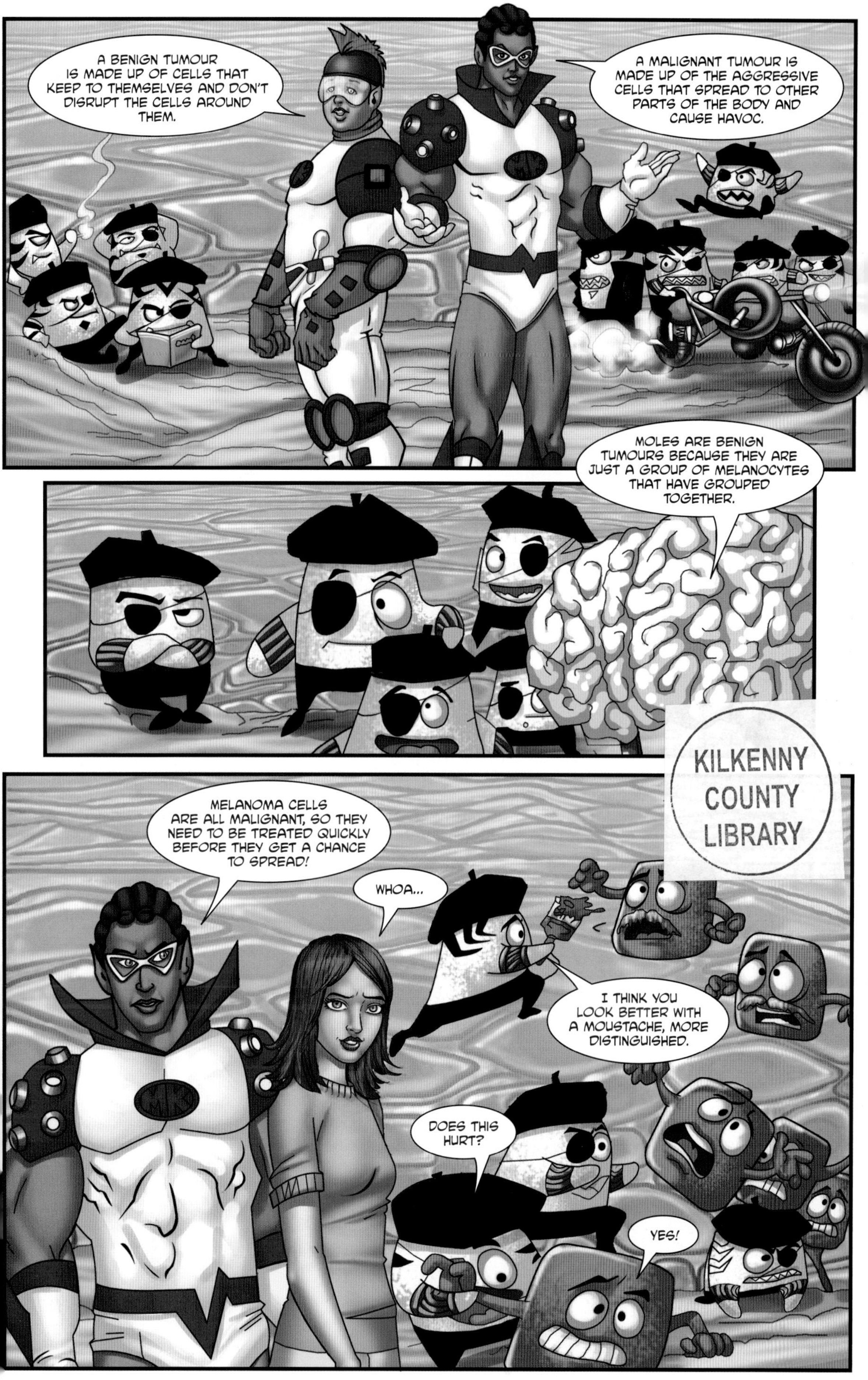
A BENIGN TUMOUR IS MADE UP OF CELLS THAT KEEP TO THEMSELVES AND DON'T DISRUPT THE CELLS AROUND THEM.
A MALIGNANT TUMOUR IS MADE UP OF THE AGGRESSIVE CELLS THAT SPREAD TO OTHER PARTS OF THE BODY AND CAUSE HAVOC.
MOLES ARE BENIGN TUMOURS BECAUSE THEY ARE JUST A GROUP OF MELANOCYTES THAT HAVE GROUPED TOGETHER.
MELANOMA CELLS ARE ALL MALIGNANT, SO THEY NEED TO BE TREATED QUICKLY BEFORE THEY GET A CHANCE TO SPREAD!
WHOA...
I THINK YOU LOOK BETTER WITH A MOUSTACHE, MORE DISTINGUISHED.
DOES THIS HURT?
YES!

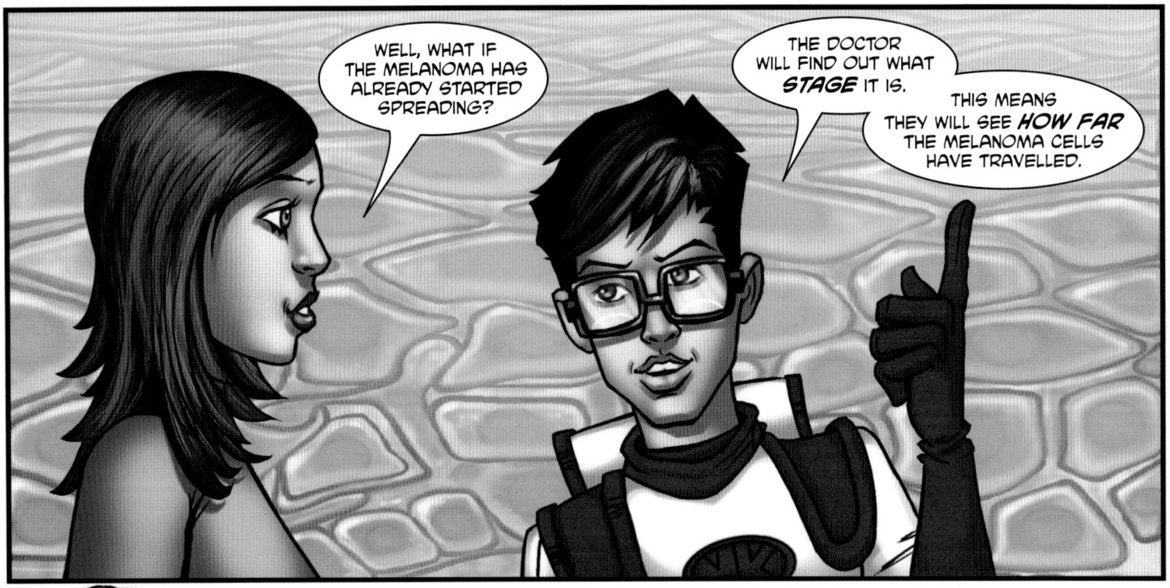
WELL, WHAT IF THE MELANOMA HAS ALREADY STARTED SPREADING?
THE DOCTOR WILL FIND OUT WHAT STAGE IT IS.
THIS MEANS THEY WILL SEE HOW FAR THE MELANOMA CELLS HAVE TRAVELLED.

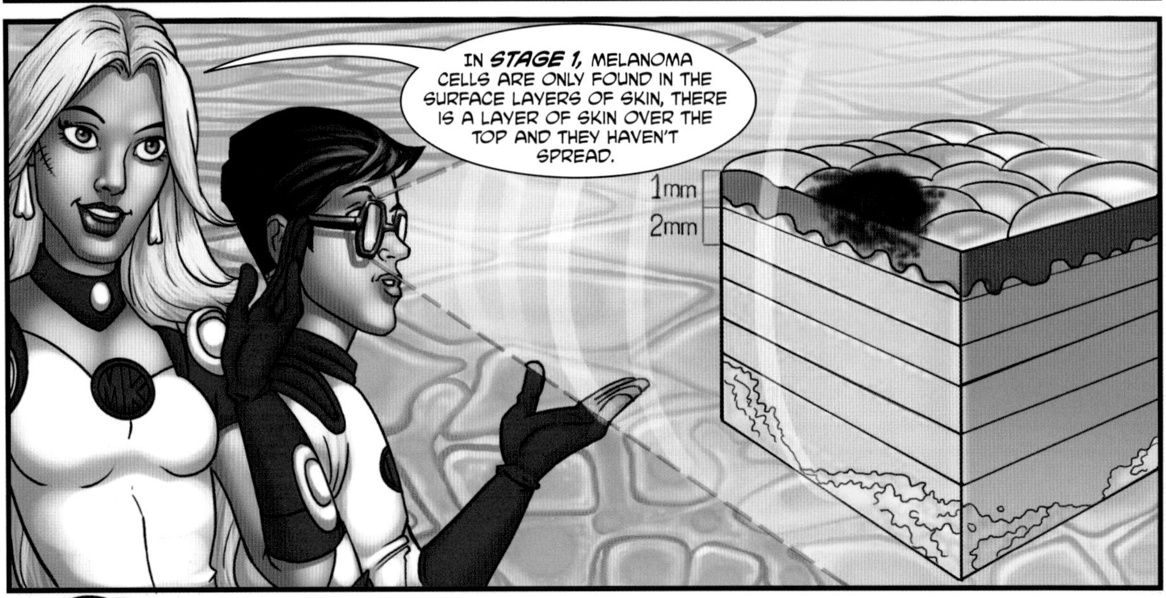
IN STAGE 1, MELANOMA CELLS ARE ONLY FOUND IN THE SURFACE LAYERS OF SKIN, THERE IS A LAYER OF SKIN OVER THE TOP AND THEY HAVEN'T SPREAD.
1mm
2mm

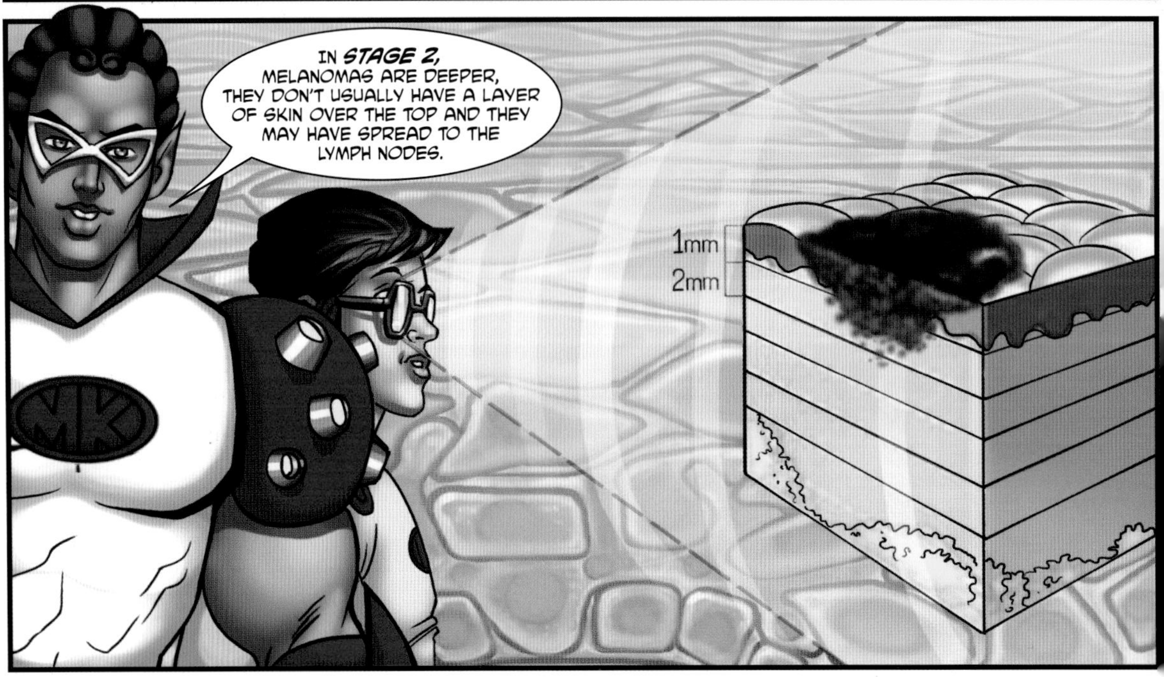
IN STAGE 2, MELANOMAS ARE DEEPER, THEY DON'T USUALLY HAVE A LAYER OF SKIN OVER THE TOP AND THEY MAY HAVE SPREAD TO THE LYMPH NODES.
1mm
2mm

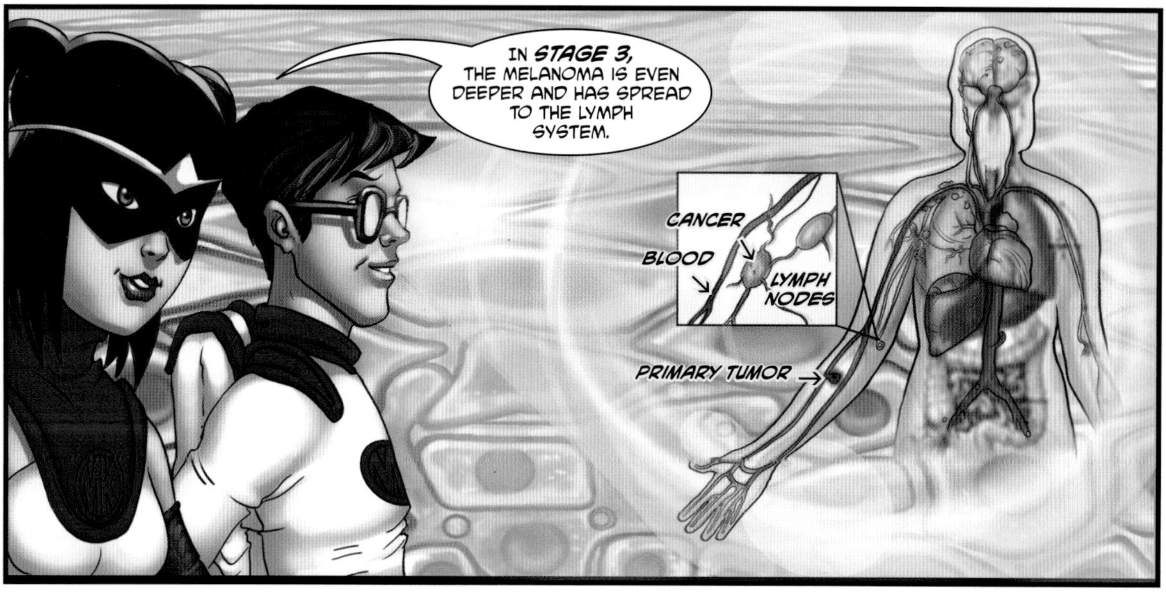
IN STAGE 3, THE MELANOMA IS EVEN DEEPER AND HAS SPREAD TO THE LYMPH SYSTEM.
CANCER
BLOOD
LYMPH NODES
PRIMARY TUMOR

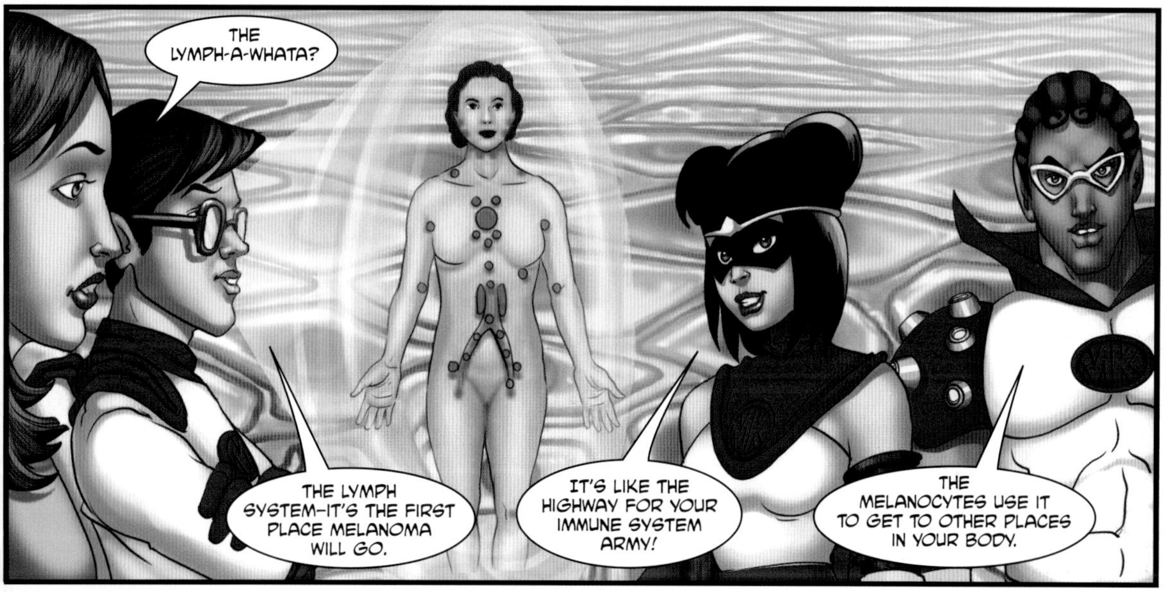
THE LYMPH-A-WHATA?
THE LYMPH SYSTEM–IT'S THE FIRST PLACE MELANOMA WILL GO.
IT'S LIKE THE HIGHWAY FOR YOUR IMMUNE SYSTEM ARMY!
THE MELANOCYTES USE IT TO GET TO OTHER PLACES IN YOUR BODY.

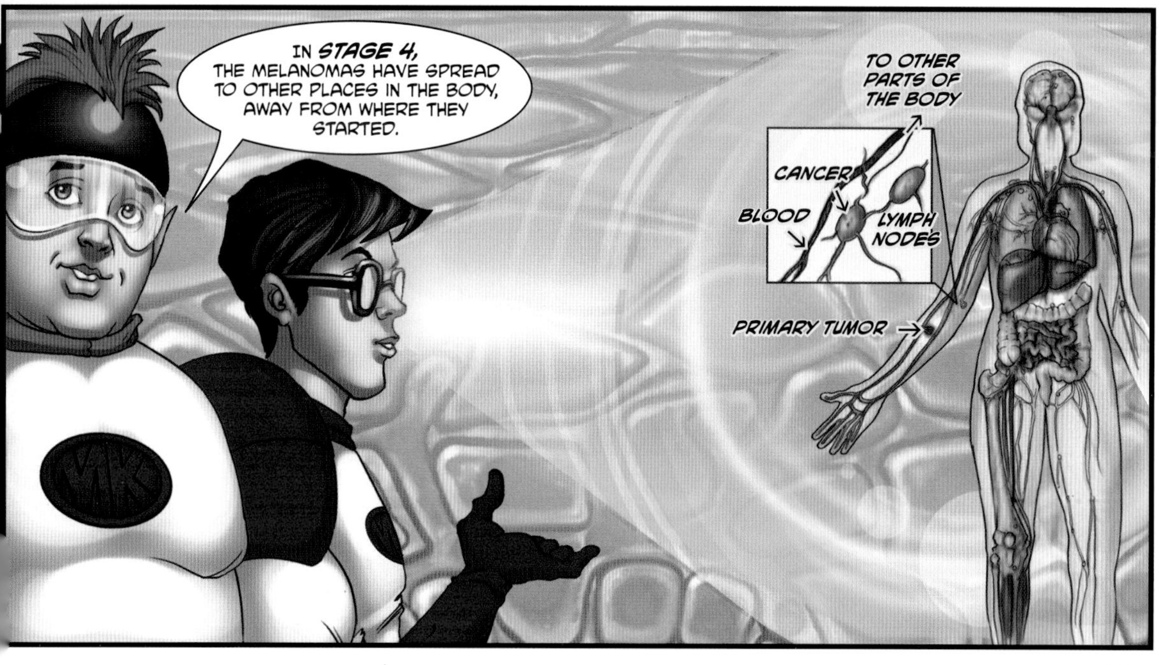
IN STAGE 4, THE MELANOMAS HAVE SPREAD TO OTHER PLACES IN THE BODY, AWAY FROM WHERE THEY STARTED.
TO OTHER PARTS OF THE BODY
CANCER
BLOOD
LYMPH NODES
PRIMARY TUMOR

SO WHAT HAPPENS NOW?
WELL, TREATMENT WILL DEPEND ON THE STAGE.
IF THE MELANOMA IS IN STAGES 1 OR 2 AN EXCISION BIOPSY WILL USUALLY CURE IT AND YOU WON'T NEED ANY MORE TREATMENT.
THIS IS MY FAVOURITE MOLE BECAUSE IT LOOKS LIKE A BRAIN!
I CAN'T BELIEVE YOU CARRY A SLIDESHOW OF MOLES WITH YOU.
OOOOH!
GIVE ME A BREAK.
THEY MIGHT HAVE TO REMOVE THE LYMPH NODE CLOSEST TO WHERE THE MELANOMA WAS JUST TO CHECK.
AND IF THE DOCTOR DOES FIND CANCER IN YOUR LYMPH NODES? WHAT THEN?

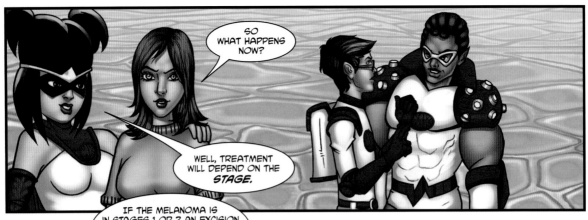

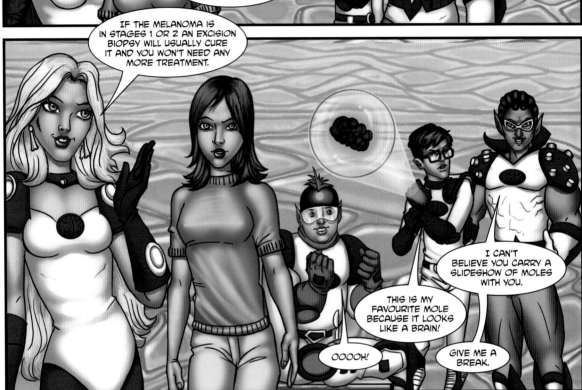

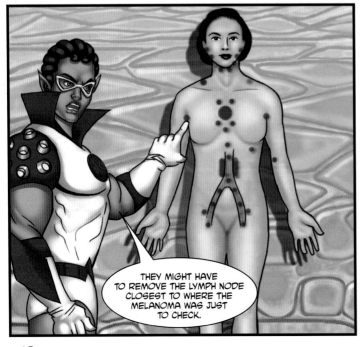

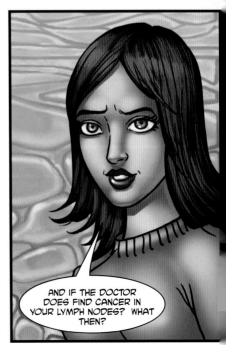

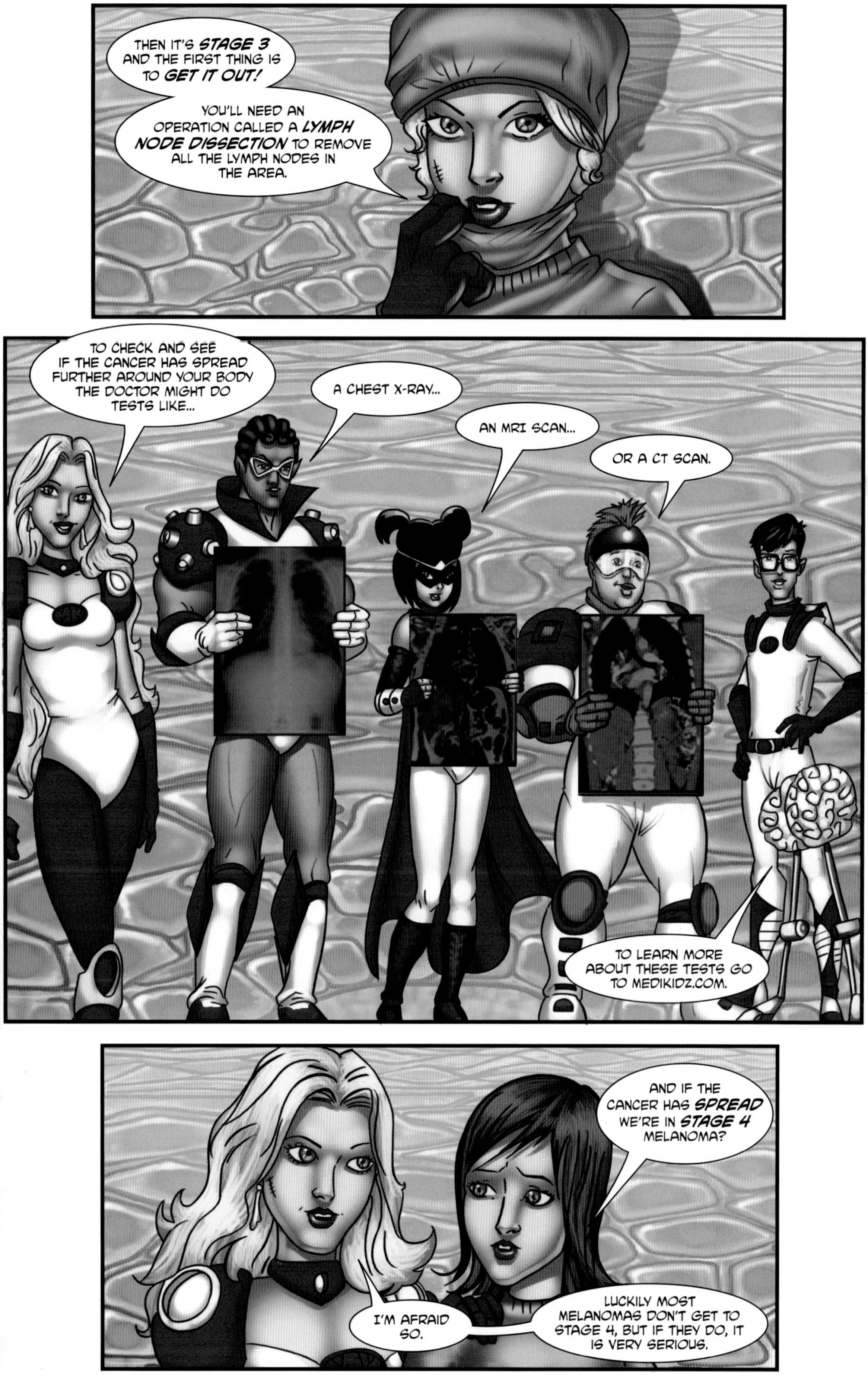
THEN IT'S STAGE 3 AND THE FIRST THING IS TO GET IT OUT!
YOU'LL NEED AN OPERATION CALLED A LYMPH NODE DISSECTION TO REMOVE ALL THE LYMPH NODES IN THE AREA.
TO CHECK AND SEE IF THE CANCER HAS SPREAD FURTHER AROUND YOUR BODY THE DOCTOR MIGHT DO TESTS LIKE...
A CHEST X-RAY...
AN MRI SCAN...
OR A CT SCAN.
TO LEARN MORE ABOUT THESE TESTS GO TO MEDIKIDZ.COM.
AND IF THE CANCER HAS SPREAD WE'RE IN STAGE 4 MELANOMA?
I'M AFRAID SO.
LUCKILY MOST MELANOMAS DON'T GET TO STAGE 4, BUT IF THEY DO, IT IS VERY SERIOUS.

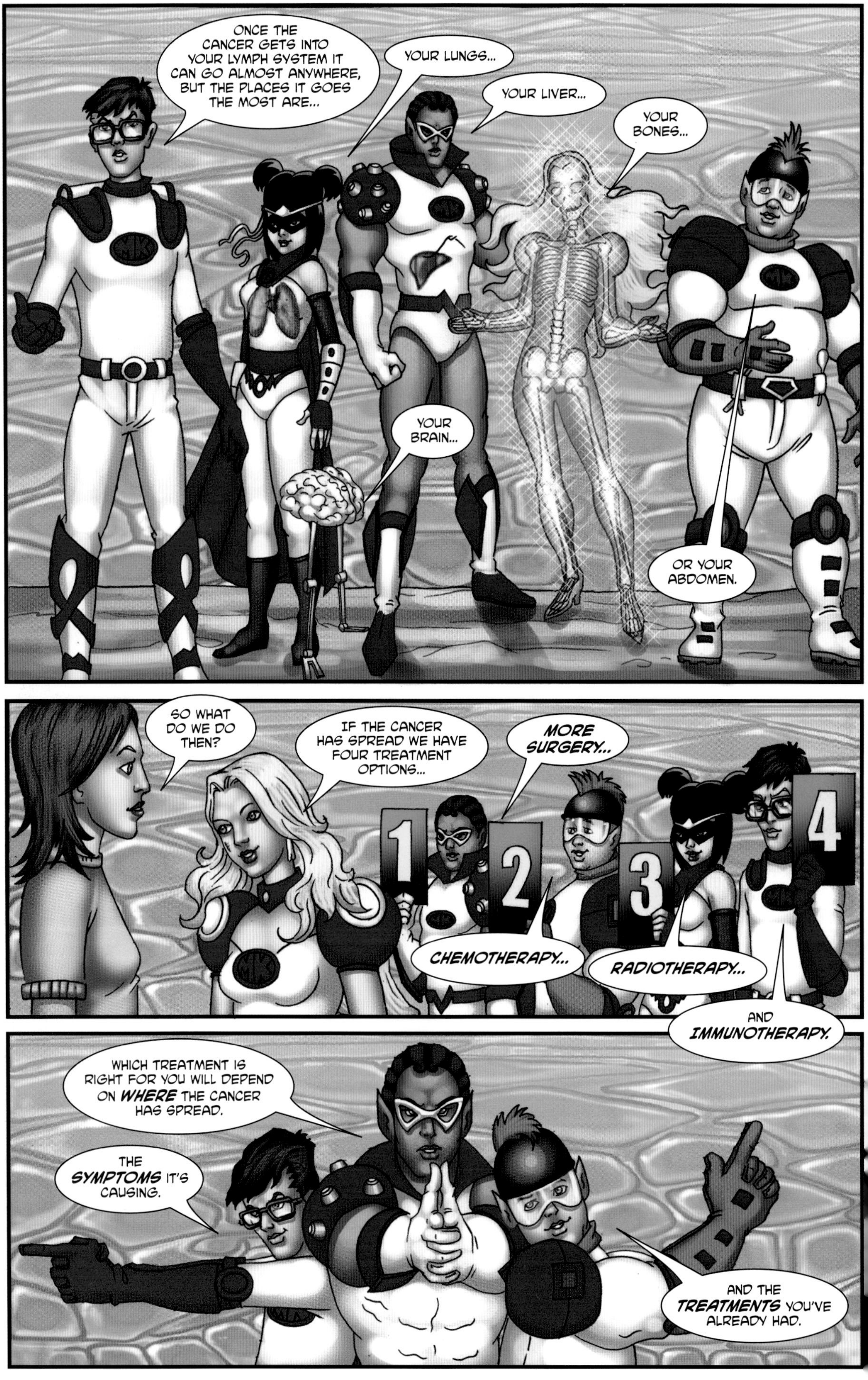
ONCE THE CANCER GETS INTO YOUR LYMPH SYSTEM IT CAN GO ALMOST ANYWHERE, BUT THE PLACES IT GOES THE MOST ARE...
YOUR LUNGS...
YOUR LIVER...
YOUR BONES...
YOUR BRAIN...
OR YOUR ABDOMEN.
SO WHAT DO WE DO THEN?
IF THE CANCER HAS SPREAD WE HAVE FOUR TREATMENT OPTIONS...
MORE SURGERY...
1
2
3
4
CHEMOTHERAPY...
RADIOTHERAPY...
AND IMMUNOTHERAPY.
WHICH TREATMENT IS RIGHT FOR YOU WILL DEPEND ON WHERE THE CANCER HAS SPREAD.
THE SYMPTOMS IT'S CAUSING.
AND THE TREATMENTS YOU'VE ALREADY HAD.

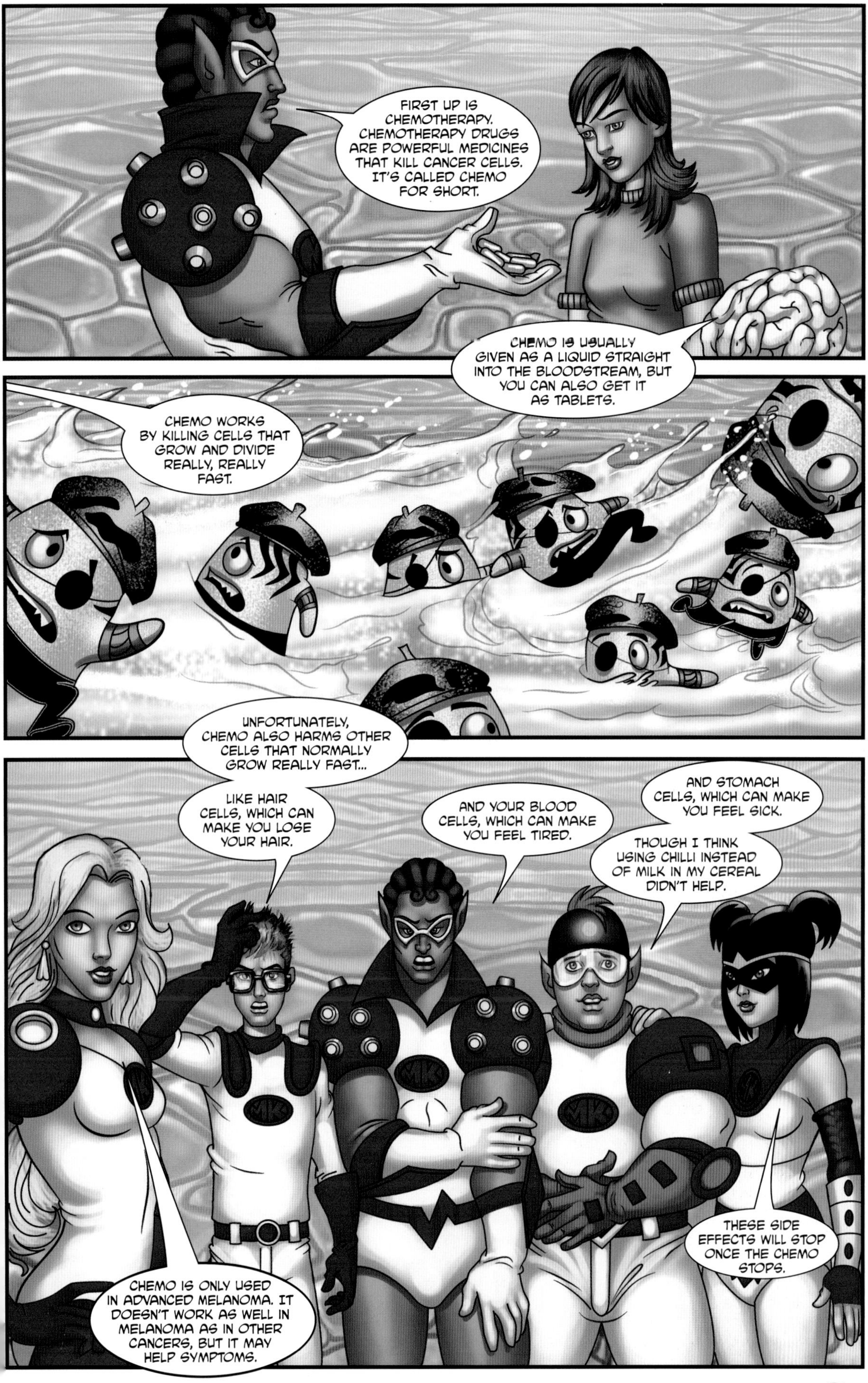
FIRST UP IS CHEMOTHERAPY. CHEMOTHERAPY DRUGS ARE POWERFUL MEDICINES THAT KILL CANCER CELLS. IT'S CALLED CHEMO FOR SHORT.
CHEMO IS USUALLY GIVEN AS A LIQUID STRAIGHT INTO THE BLOODSTREAM, BUT YOU CAN ALSO GET IT AS TABLETS.
CHEMO WORKS BY KILLING CELLS THAT GROW AND DIVIDE REALLY, REALLY FAST.
UNFORTUNATELY, CHEMO ALSO HARMS OTHER CELLS THAT NORMALLY GROW REALLY FAST...
LIKE HAIR CELLS, WHICH CAN MAKE YOU LOSE YOUR HAIR.
AND YOUR BLOOD CELLS, WHICH CAN MAKE YOU FEEL TIRED.
AND STOMACH CELLS, WHICH CAN MAKE YOU FEEL SICK.
THOUGH I THINK USING CHILLI INSTEAD OF MILK IN MY CEREAL DIDN'T HELP.
THESE SIDE EFFECTS WILL STOP ONCE THE CHEMO STOPS.
CHEMO IS ONLY USED IN ADVANCED MELANOMA. IT DOESN'T WORK AS WELL IN MELANOMA AS IN OTHER CANCERS, BUT IT MAY HELP SYMPTOMS.

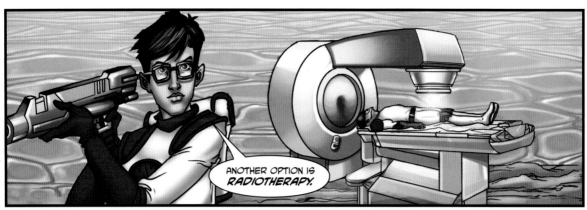

ANOTHER OPTION IS *RADIOTHERAPY.*

RADIOTHERAPY USES VERY POWERFUL ENERGY BEAMS TO KILL CANCER CELLS.

RUN!

DEATH COMES FROM ABOVE!

IT WORKS BY ZAPPING THE 'CELLS BEHAVING BADLY'.

MUMMY.

IT ONLY TAKES A FEW MINUTES, BUT YOU MIGHT HAVE TO HAVE IT DONE EVERY DAY FOR A FEW WEEKS.

SOMETIMES RADIOTHERAPY CAN BE DONE IN A SINGLE DAY, USING REALLY REALLY STRONG RADIATION BEAMS. THIS IS CALLED *RADIOSURGERY.*

ZAP!

RADIOTHERAPY TO THE SKIN DOESN'T HAVE MANY SIDE EFFECTS.

BUT, YOUR SKIN CAN BECOME SLIGHTLY RED AND SORE.

HEY, I SAID IT WAS SORE!

IF YOU HAVE THE TREATMENT IN OTHER AREAS IT CAN MAKE YOU FEEL TIRED AND SICK.

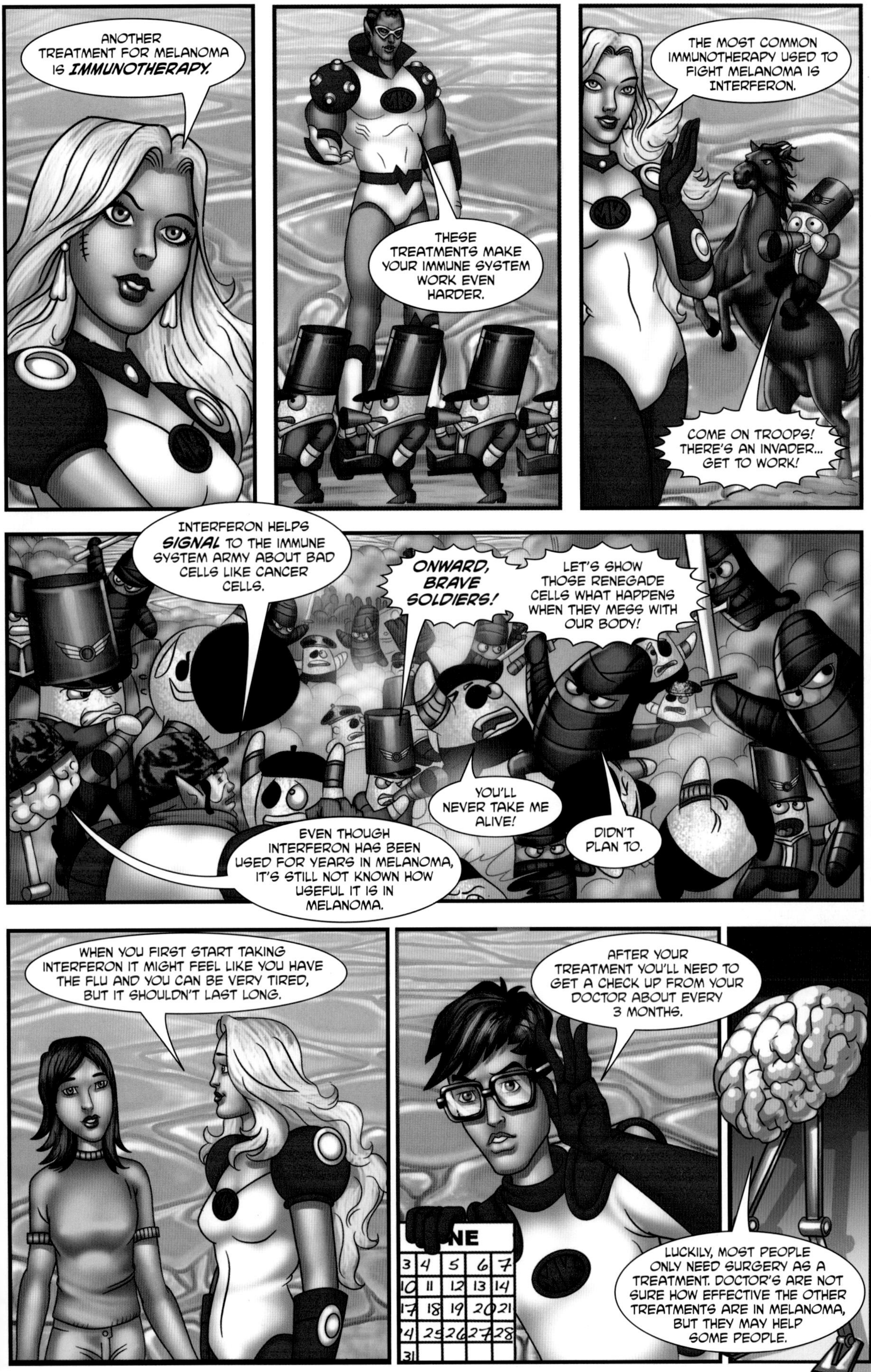
ANOTHER TREATMENT FOR MELANOMA IS IMMUNOTHERAPY.
THESE TREATMENTS MAKE YOUR IMMUNE SYSTEM WORK EVEN HARDER.
THE MOST COMMON IMMUNOTHERAPY USED TO FIGHT MELANOMA IS INTERFERON.
COME ON TROOPS! THERE'S AN INVADER... GET TO WORK!
INTERFERON HELPS SIGNAL TO THE IMMUNE SYSTEM ARMY ABOUT BAD CELLS LIKE CANCER CELLS.
ONWARD, BRAVE SOLDIERS!
LET'S SHOW THOSE RENEGADE CELLS WHAT HAPPENS WHEN THEY MESS WITH OUR BODY!
YOU'LL NEVER TAKE ME ALIVE!
DIDN'T PLAN TO.
EVEN THOUGH INTERFERON HAS BEEN USED FOR YEARS IN MELANOMA, IT'S STILL NOT KNOWN HOW USEFUL IT IS IN MELANOMA.
WHEN YOU FIRST START TAKING INTERFERON IT MIGHT FEEL LIKE YOU HAVE THE FLU AND YOU CAN BE VERY TIRED, BUT IT SHOULDN'T LAST LONG.
AFTER YOUR TREATMENT YOU'LL NEED TO GET A CHECK UP FROM YOUR DOCTOR ABOUT EVERY 3 MONTHS.
LUCKILY, MOST PEOPLE ONLY NEED SURGERY AS A TREATMENT. DOCTOR'S ARE NOT SURE HOW EFFECTIVE THE OTHER TREATMENTS ARE IN MELANOMA, BUT THEY MAY HELP SOME PEOPLE.

BUT, WHY DAD? WHY DID HE HAVE TO GET MELANOMA?

GETTING LOTS OF SUN OR USING SUNBEDS IS THE MAIN THING THAT INCREASES YOUR CHANCE OF GETTING MELANOMA.

IT'S REALLY BEAMING DOWN TODAY.

WE NEED MORE MELANIN!

DOUBLE TIME, BOYS!

WHOA!

WHEN YOU GET LOTS OF SUN YOUR MELANOCYTES WORK OVERTIME TO MAKE ENOUGH MELANIN TO PROTECT YOUR SKIN.

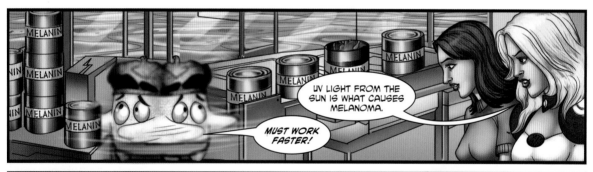

UV LIGHT FROM THE SUN IS WHAT CAUSES MELANOMA.

MUST WORK FASTER!

TOO MUCH WORK CAN DAMAGE AND STRESS THE MEL'S OUT!

IT'S TOO MUCH! I DON'T GET PAID ENOUGH FOR THIS!

THIS IS WHAT CAUSES THE MEL'S TO START BEHAVING BADLY!

IT FEELS GOOD TO BE BAD!

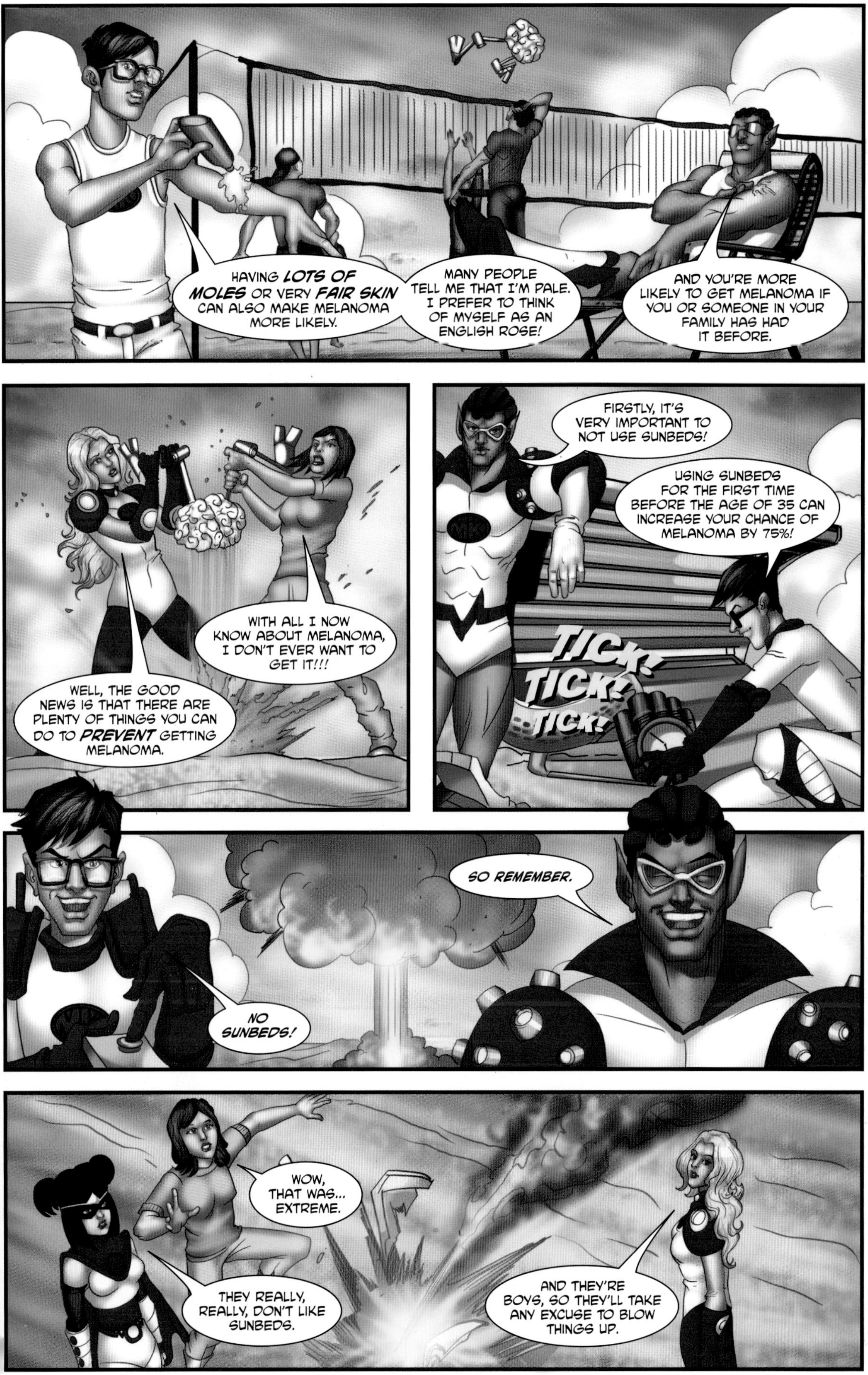
HAVING LOTS OF MOLES OR VERY FAIR SKIN CAN ALSO MAKE MELANOMA MORE LIKELY.
MANY PEOPLE TELL ME THAT I'M PALE. I PREFER TO THINK OF MYSELF AS AN ENGLISH ROSE!
AND YOU'RE MORE LIKELY TO GET MELANOMA IF YOU OR SOMEONE IN YOUR FAMILY HAS HAD IT BEFORE.
WITH ALL I NOW KNOW ABOUT MELANOMA, I DON'T EVER WANT TO GET IT!!!
WELL, THE GOOD NEWS IS THAT THERE ARE PLENTY OF THINGS YOU CAN DO TO PREVENT GETTING MELANOMA.
FIRSTLY, IT'S VERY IMPORTANT TO NOT USE SUNBEDS!
USING SUNBEDS FOR THE FIRST TIME BEFORE THE AGE OF 35 CAN INCREASE YOUR CHANCE OF MELANOMA BY 75%!
TICK! TICK! TICK!
SO REMEMBER.
NO SUNBEDS!
WOW, THAT WAS... EXTREME.
THEY REALLY, REALLY, DON'T LIKE SUNBEDS.
AND THEY'RE BOYS, SO THEY'LL TAKE ANY EXCUSE TO BLOW THINGS UP.

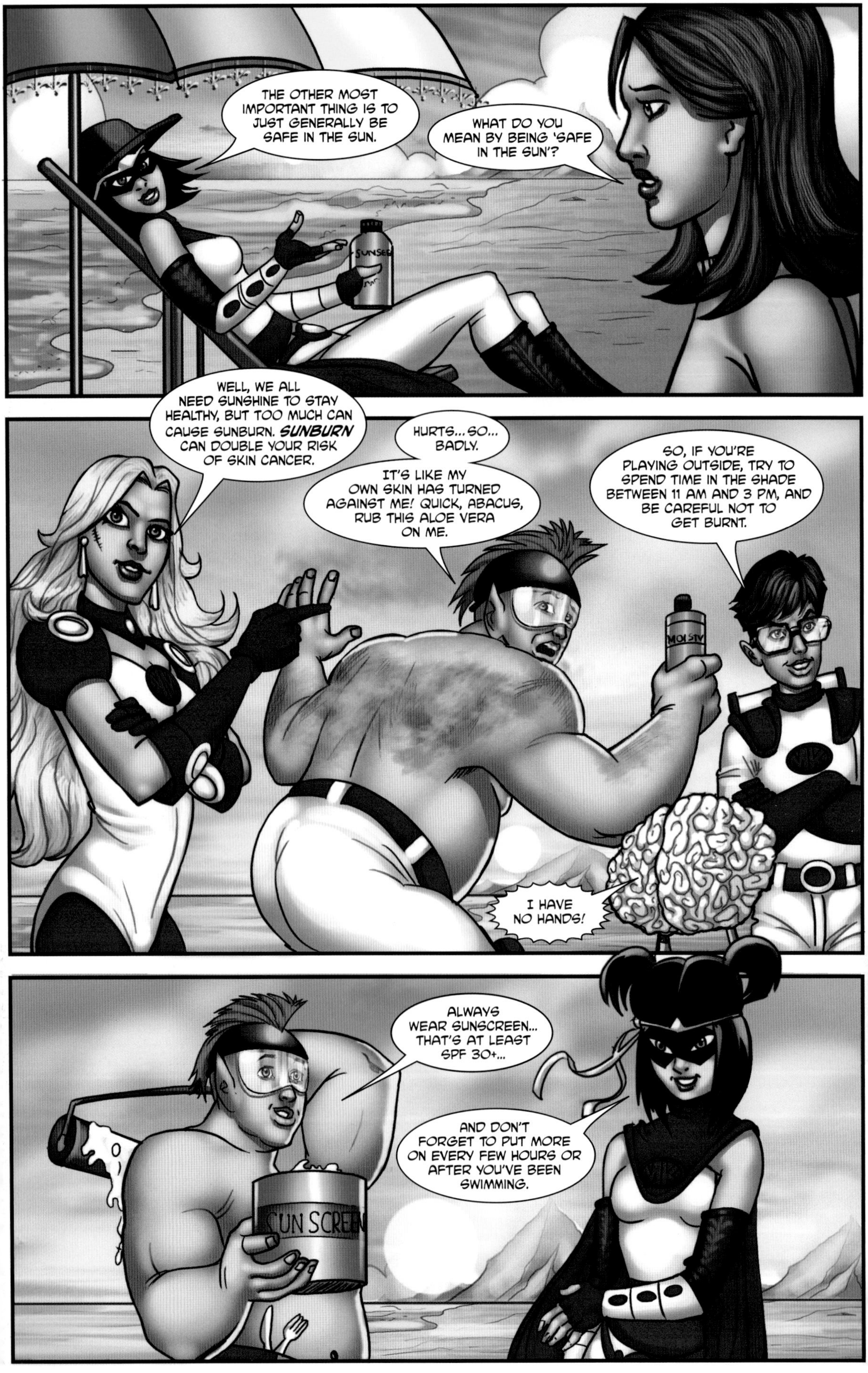
THE OTHER MOST IMPORTANT THING IS TO JUST GENERALLY BE SAFE IN THE SUN.
WHAT DO YOU MEAN BY BEING 'SAFE IN THE SUN'?
WELL, WE ALL NEED SUNSHINE TO STAY HEALTHY, BUT TOO MUCH CAN CAUSE SUNBURN. ***SUNBURN*** CAN DOUBLE YOUR RISK OF SKIN CANCER.
HURTS... SO... BADLY.
IT'S LIKE MY OWN SKIN HAS TURNED AGAINST ME! QUICK, ABACUS, RUB THIS ALOE VERA ON ME.
SO, IF YOU'RE PLAYING OUTSIDE, TRY TO SPEND TIME IN THE SHADE BETWEEN 11 AM AND 3 PM, AND BE CAREFUL NOT TO GET BURNT.
I HAVE NO HANDS!
ALWAYS WEAR SUNSCREEN... THAT'S AT LEAST SPF 30+...
AND DON'T FORGET TO PUT MORE ON EVERY FEW HOURS OR AFTER YOU'VE BEEN SWIMMING.
SUN SCREEN

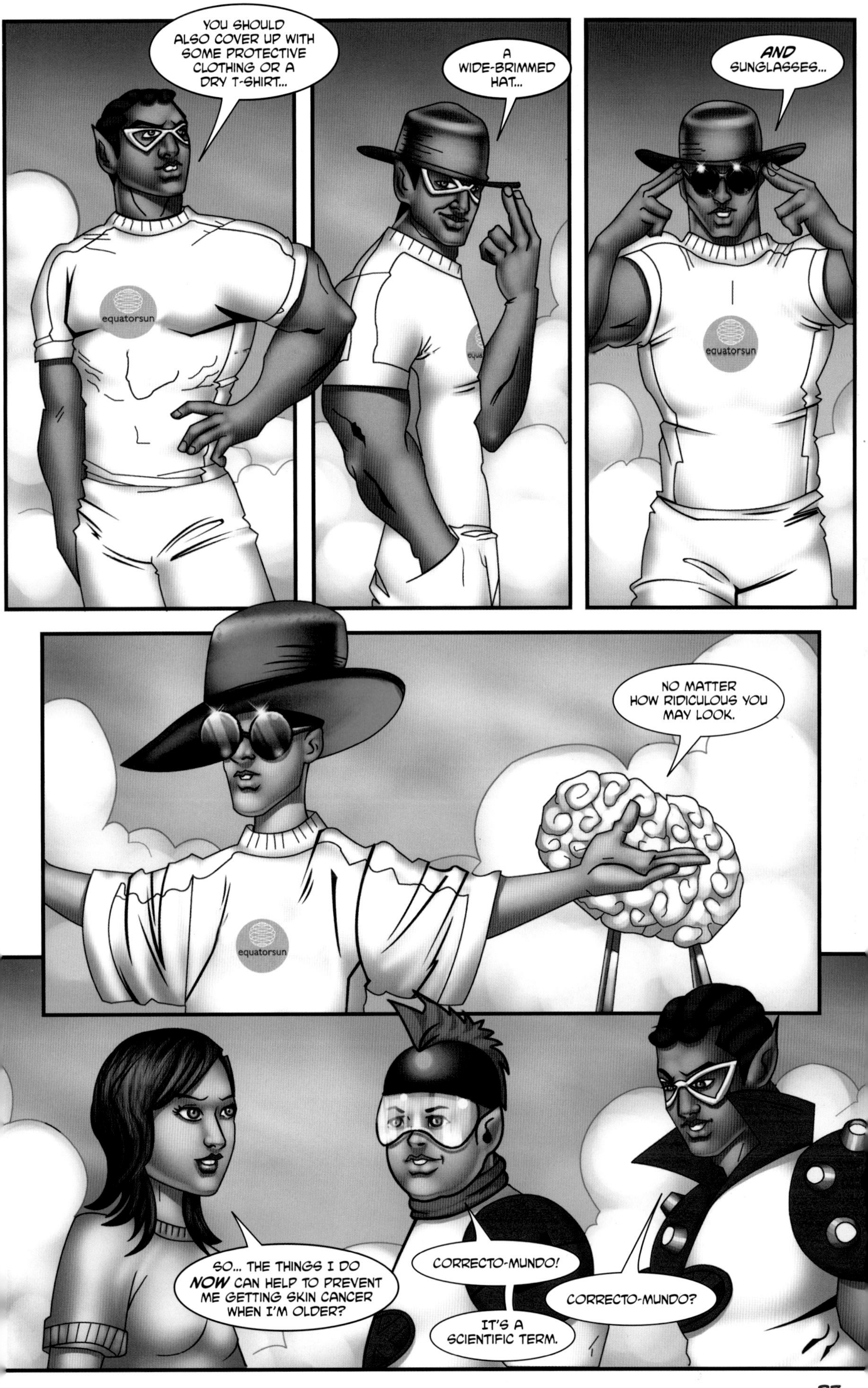
YOU SHOULD ALSO COVER UP WITH SOME PROTECTIVE CLOTHING OR A DRY T-SHIRT...
equatorsun
A WIDE-BRIMMED HAT...
AND SUNGLASSES...
equatorsun
NO MATTER HOW RIDICULOUS YOU MAY LOOK.
equatorsun
SO... THE THINGS I DO NOW CAN HELP TO PREVENT ME GETTING SKIN CANCER WHEN I'M OLDER?
CORRECTO-MUNDO!
CORRECTO-MUNDO?
IT'S A SCIENTIFIC TERM.

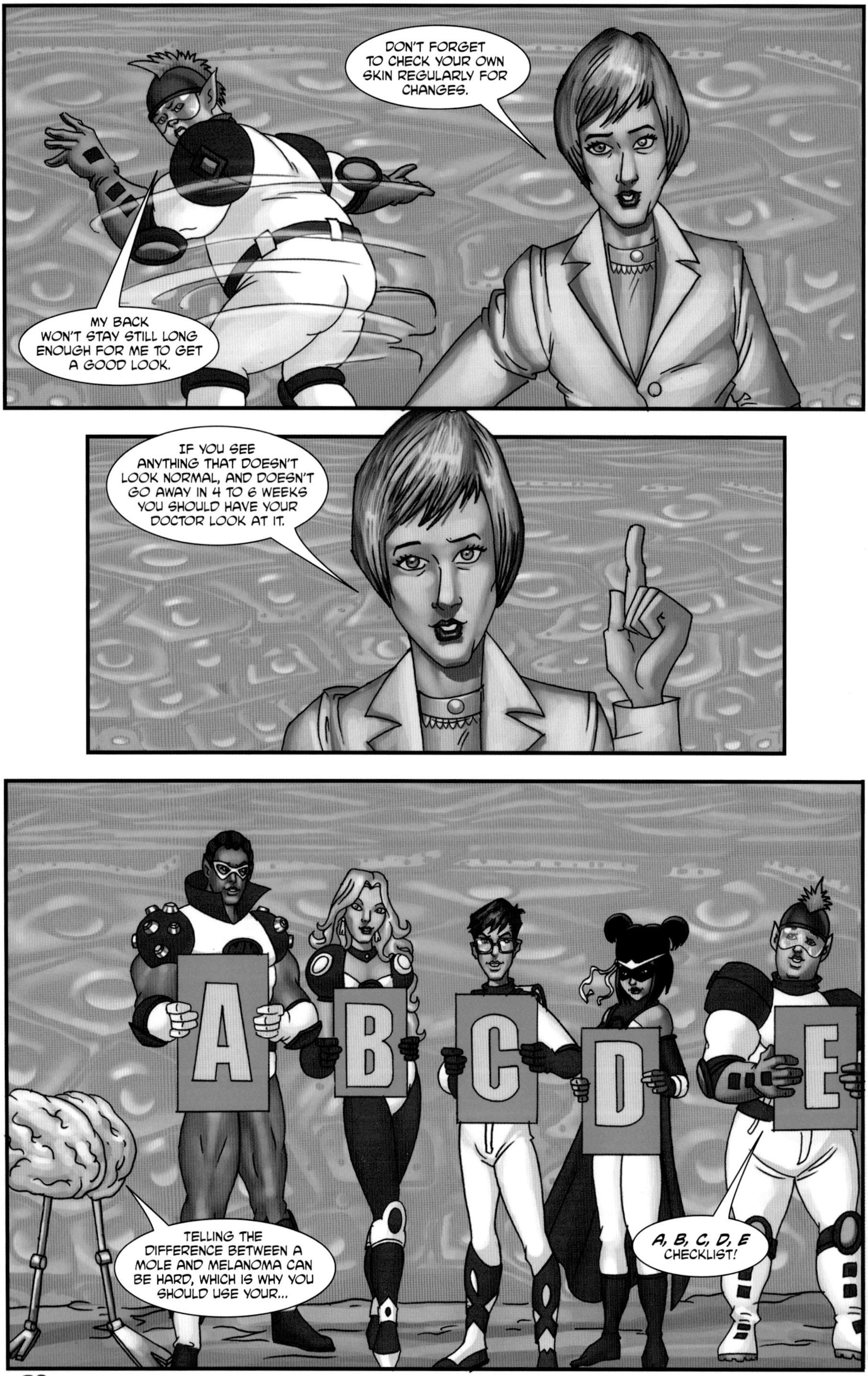
DON'T FORGET TO CHECK YOUR OWN SKIN REGULARLY FOR CHANGES.
MY BACK WON'T STAY STILL LONG ENOUGH FOR ME TO GET A GOOD LOOK.
IF YOU SEE ANYTHING THAT DOESN'T LOOK NORMAL, AND DOESN'T GO AWAY IN 4 TO 6 WEEKS YOU SHOULD HAVE YOUR DOCTOR LOOK AT IT.
A
B
C
D
E
TELLING THE DIFFERENCE BETWEEN A MOLE AND MELANOMA CAN BE HARD, WHICH IS WHY YOU SHOULD USE YOUR...
A, B, C, D, E CHECKLIST!

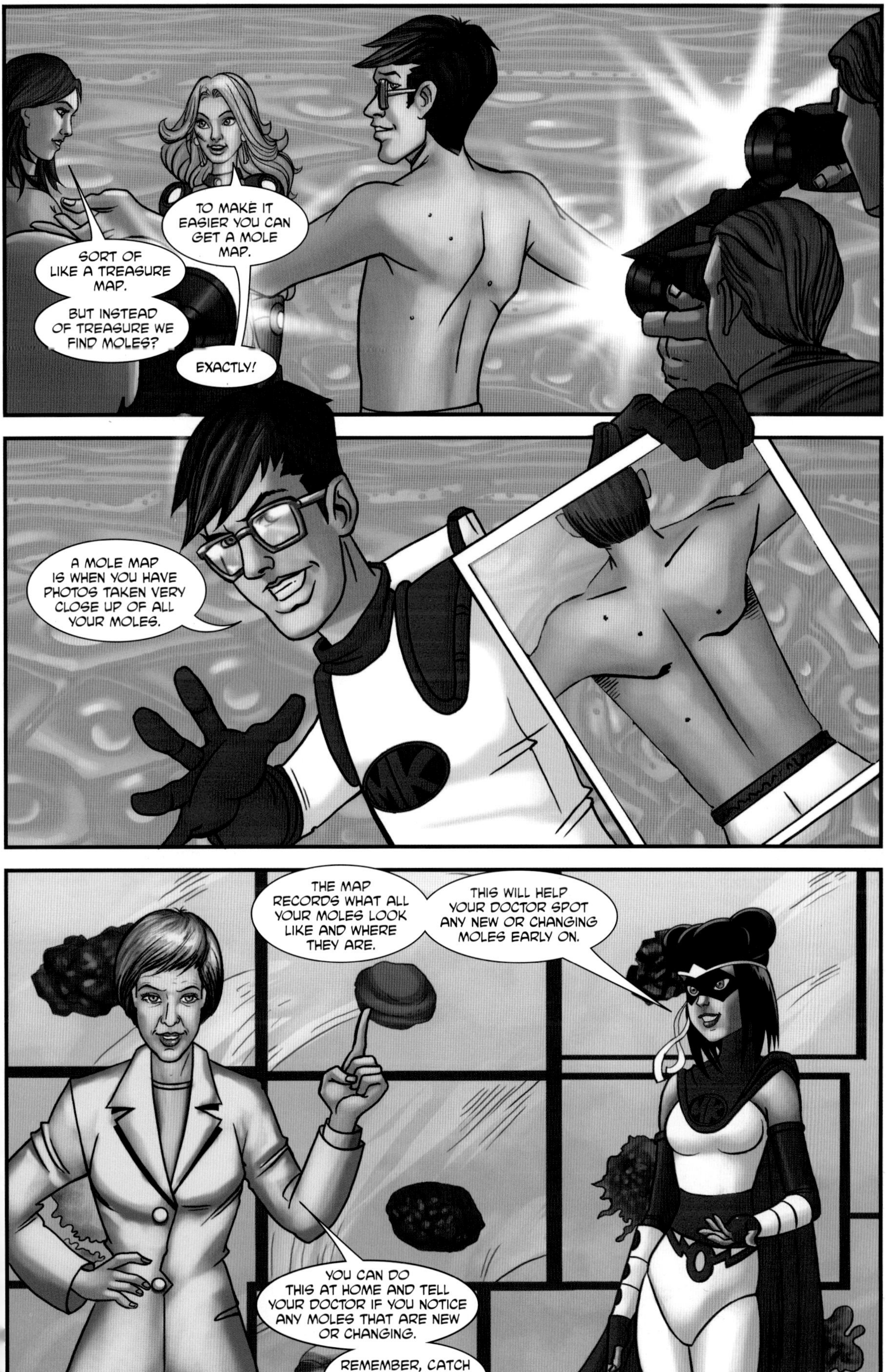

SORT OF LIKE A TREASURE MAP.
BUT INSTEAD OF TREASURE WE FIND MOLES?
TO MAKE IT EASIER YOU CAN GET A MOLE MAP.
EXACTLY!
A MOLE MAP IS WHEN YOU HAVE PHOTOS TAKEN VERY CLOSE UP OF ALL YOUR MOLES.
THE MAP RECORDS WHAT ALL YOUR MOLES LOOK LIKE AND WHERE THEY ARE.
THIS WILL HELP YOUR DOCTOR SPOT ANY NEW OR CHANGING MOLES EARLY ON.
YOU CAN DO THIS AT HOME AND TELL YOUR DOCTOR IF YOU NOTICE ANY MOLES THAT ARE NEW OR CHANGING.
REMEMBER, CATCH 'EM QUICK, TO GIVE 'EM THE FLICK!

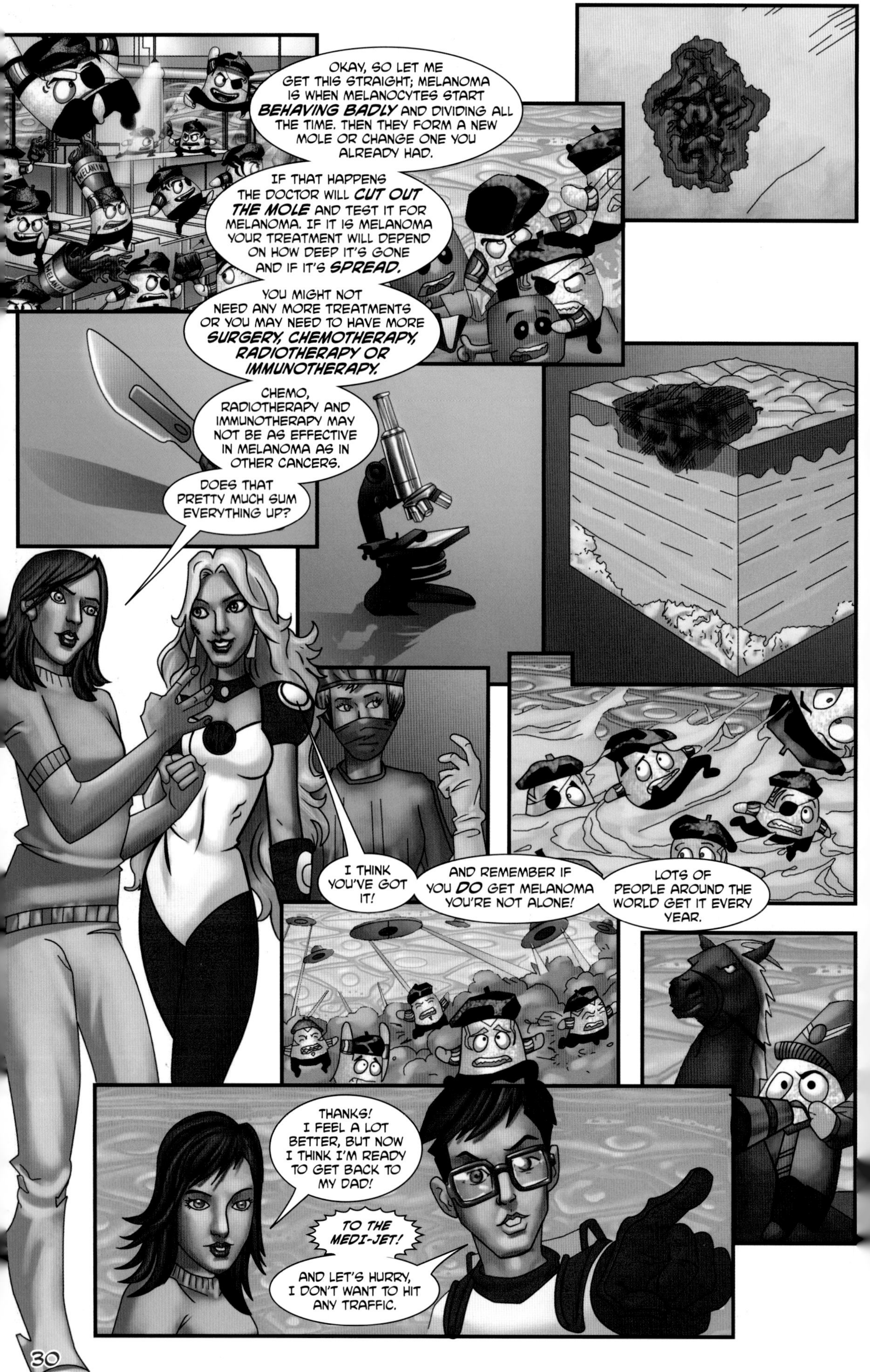
OKAY, SO LET ME GET THIS STRAIGHT; MELANOMA IS WHEN MELANOCYTES START BEHAVING BADLY AND DIVIDING ALL THE TIME. THEN THEY FORM A NEW MOLE OR CHANGE ONE YOU ALREADY HAD.
IF THAT HAPPENS THE DOCTOR WILL CUT OUT THE MOLE AND TEST IT FOR MELANOMA. IF IT IS MELANOMA YOUR TREATMENT WILL DEPEND ON HOW DEEP IT'S GONE AND IF IT'S SPREAD.
YOU MIGHT NOT NEED ANY MORE TREATMENTS OR YOU MAY NEED TO HAVE MORE SURGERY, CHEMOTHERAPY, RADIOTHERAPY OR IMMUNOTHERAPY.
CHEMO, RADIOTHERAPY AND IMMUNOTHERAPY MAY NOT BE AS EFFECTIVE IN MELANOMA AS IN OTHER CANCERS.
DOES THAT PRETTY MUCH SUM EVERYTHING UP?
I THINK YOU'VE GOT IT!
AND REMEMBER IF YOU DO GET MELANOMA YOU'RE NOT ALONE!
LOTS OF PEOPLE AROUND THE WORLD GET IT EVERY YEAR.
THANKS! I FEEL A LOT BETTER, BUT NOW I THINK I'M READY TO GET BACK TO MY DAD!
TO THE MEDI-JET!
AND LET'S HURRY, I DON'T WANT TO HIT ANY TRAFFIC.

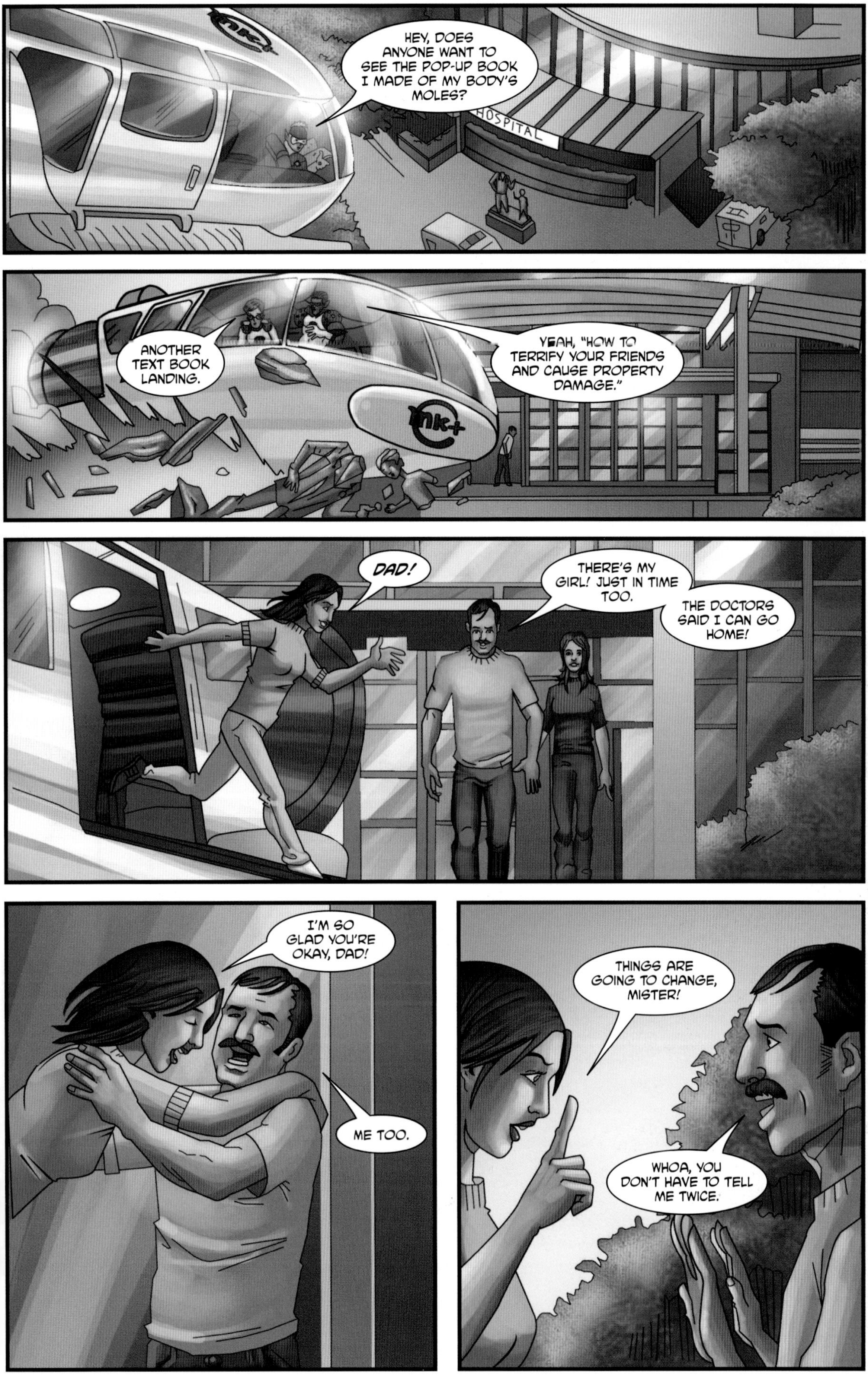

HEY, DOES ANYONE WANT TO SEE THE POP-UP BOOK I MADE OF MY BODY'S MOLES?
HOSPITAL
ANOTHER TEXT BOOK LANDING.
YEAH, "HOW TO TERRIFY YOUR FRIENDS AND CAUSE PROPERTY DAMAGE."
DAD!
THERE'S MY GIRL! JUST IN TIME TOO.
THE DOCTORS SAID I CAN GO HOME!
I'M SO GLAD YOU'RE OKAY, DAD!
ME TOO.
THINGS ARE GOING TO CHANGE, MISTER!
WHOA, YOU DON'T HAVE TO TELL ME TWICE.

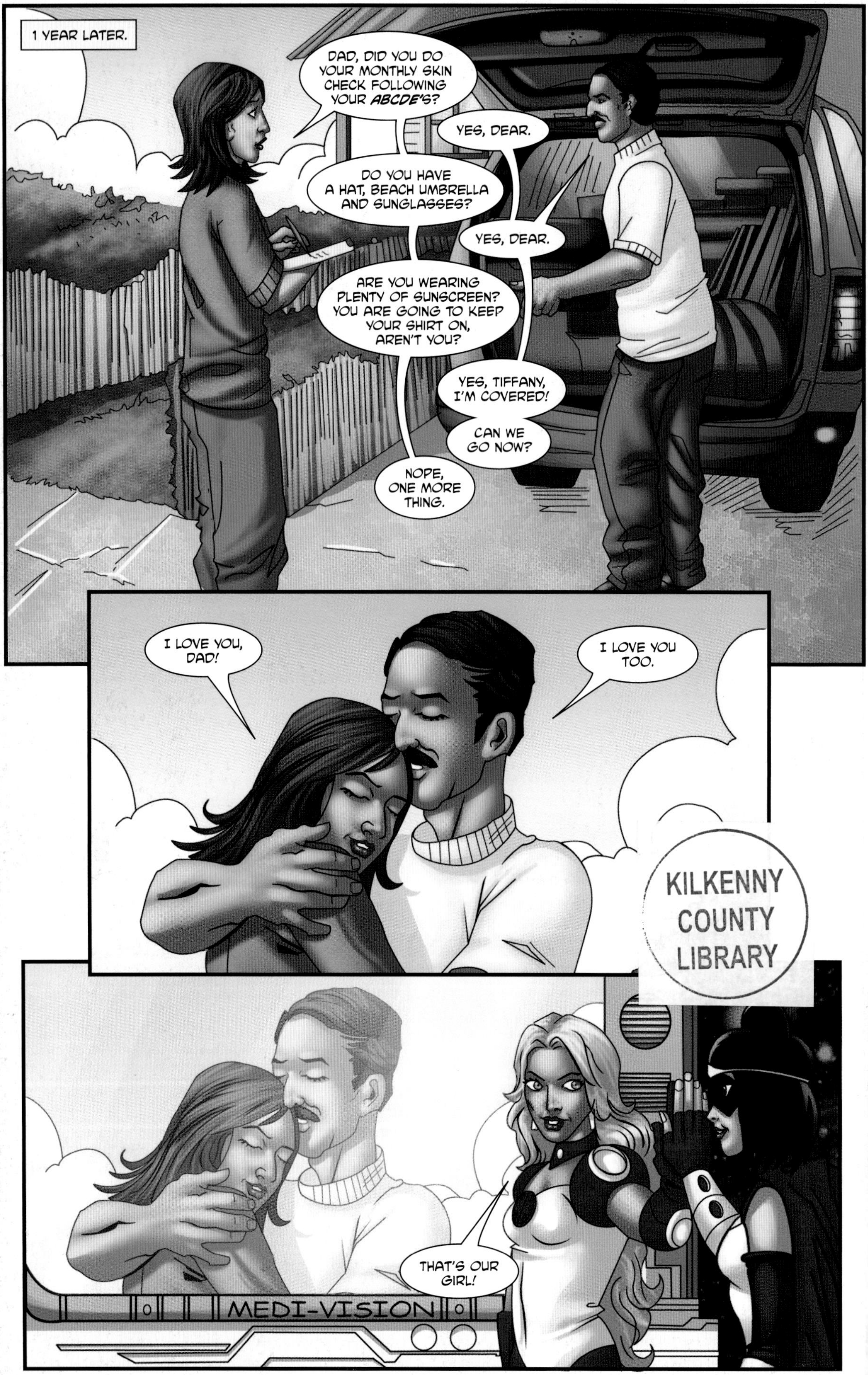
1 YEAR LATER.
DAD, DID YOU DO YOUR MONTHLY SKIN CHECK FOLLOWING YOUR ABCDE'S?
YES, DEAR.
DO YOU HAVE A HAT, BEACH UMBRELLA AND SUNGLASSES?
YES, DEAR.
ARE YOU WEARING PLENTY OF SUNSCREEN? YOU ARE GOING TO KEEP YOUR SHIRT ON, AREN'T YOU?
YES, TIFFANY, I'M COVERED!
CAN WE GO NOW?
NOPE, ONE MORE THING.
I LOVE YOU, DAD!
I LOVE YOU TOO.
MEDI-VISION
THAT'S OUR GIRL!